Houghton Mifflin

ENJOY

LITERACY ACTIVITY BOOK

Senior Authors
J. David Cooper
John J. Pikulski

Authors
Kathryn H. Au
Margarita Calderón
Jacqueline C. Comas
Marjorie Y. Lipson
J. Sabrina Mims
Susan E. Page
Sheila W. Valencia
MaryEllen Vogt

Consultants
Dolores Malcolm
Tina Saldivar
Shane Templeton

Houghton Mifflin Company • Boston

Atlanta • Dallas • Geneva, Illinois • Palo Alto • Princeton

Illustration Credits
Susan Aiello 54, 78, 94, 108, 109; Elizabeth Allen 17, 29, 57, 81, 113; Shirley Beckes 114, 120; Ruth Brunke 66, 92, 97, 98, 106; Robert Burger/Deborah Wolfe 20, 83; Tony Caldwell/Cornell & McCarthy 61, 62; Estelle Carol/HK Portfolio 33; Olivia Cole/Asciutto Art Reps 74, 115; Ruta Daugavietis 7, 8, 70; Susanne Demarco/Asciutto Art Reps 13; Tom Duckworth 19, 24, 69, 71, 73, 82, 93, 95, 119, 122; Tom Durfee/Steven Edsey 11, 29, 38, 39; George Eisner/Steven Edsey 88; Bryan Friel/Steven Edsey 25; Dave Garbot 2, 9, 28, 35; Patrick Girouard 50, 80; Bob Lange 4, 67, 68, 75, 99, 102; Bert Mayse 12, 21, 49, 55, 59, 63, 79; Judith Moffatt 47, 51, 52, 57; Deborah Morse 32; Lynn Sweat/Cornell & McCarthy 26, 34; George Ulrich/HK Portfolio 46; Dave Winter 38, 118, 123.

Photo Credits
©Adamsmith Productions/H. Armstrong Roberts, Inc. 90; ©Alinari/Art Resource, NY 105; ©A.W. Ambler from National Audubon Society/Photo Researchers, Inc. 36, bottom left; ©Don Clark/Grant Heilman Photography 15, center left; ©Paul Dance/Tony Stone Images 47; ©Jack Dermid from National Audubon Society/Photo Researchers, Inc. 36, top right; ©H. Armstrong Roberts, Inc. 53, right; ©Hal Harrison/Grant Heilman Photography 36, top left; ©Grant Heilman Photography 15, center right, bottom; ©Breck P. Kent/Animals Animals 97; ©R. Kord/H. Armstrong Roberts, Inc. 53, left; Photograph ©1985 by Jill Krementz 116; ©Michael Newman/PhotoEdit 77; ©PhotoDisc 48, 52, 56, 60; ©Photo Researchers, Inc. 101; ©Alan Pitcairn/Grant Heilman Photography 22; ©Leonard Lee Rue III/Tony Stone Images 117, top right; ©Runk/Shoenberger from Grant Heilman Photography 36, bottom right; ©John Shannon from National Audubon Society/Photo Researchers, Inc. 15, top left; ©Jerome Wexler/Photo Researchers, Inc. 15, top right; All other photographs by Ralph J. Brunke Photography.

1997 Impression

Printed in the U.S.A.

ISBN: 0-395-72484-8

23 24 25 26 27 28-HS-07 06 05 04

CONTENTS

CONTENTS

Name

My Reading Strategy Guide

As I read, do I **predict/infer** by . . .	
Looking for important information?	☐
Looking at illustrations?	☐
Thinking about what I know?	☐
Thinking about what will happen next or what I want to learn?	☐
As I read, do I self-question by . . .	
Asking questions to answer for myself as I go along?	☐
As I read, do I think about words by . . .	
Figuring out words by using context, sounds, and word parts?	☐
As I read, do I monitor by asking . . .	
Does this make sense to me?	☐
Does it help me meet my purpose?	☐
Do I try fix-ups:	
• Reread	☐
• Read ahead	☐
• Look at illustrations	☐
• Ask for help	☐
Do I summarize, both while I read and after reading by . . .	
Thinking about story parts?	☐
Thinking about main ideas and important details?	☐
As I read, do I evaluate by . . .	
Asking myself how I feel about what I read?	☐
Asking myself if this could really happen?	☐

Name

Dear Friend

Imagine you are a teacher. Your class is full of students who behave very badly. One day a police detective visits your class. The students are horrible. Write a letter to your friend telling about the detective's visit to your class. Use each vocabulary word in your letter.

misbehaving	detective	worst-behaved	change
act up	rapped	secret	

Name

Where Did She Go?

Complete the story map about *Miss Nelson Is Missing!*

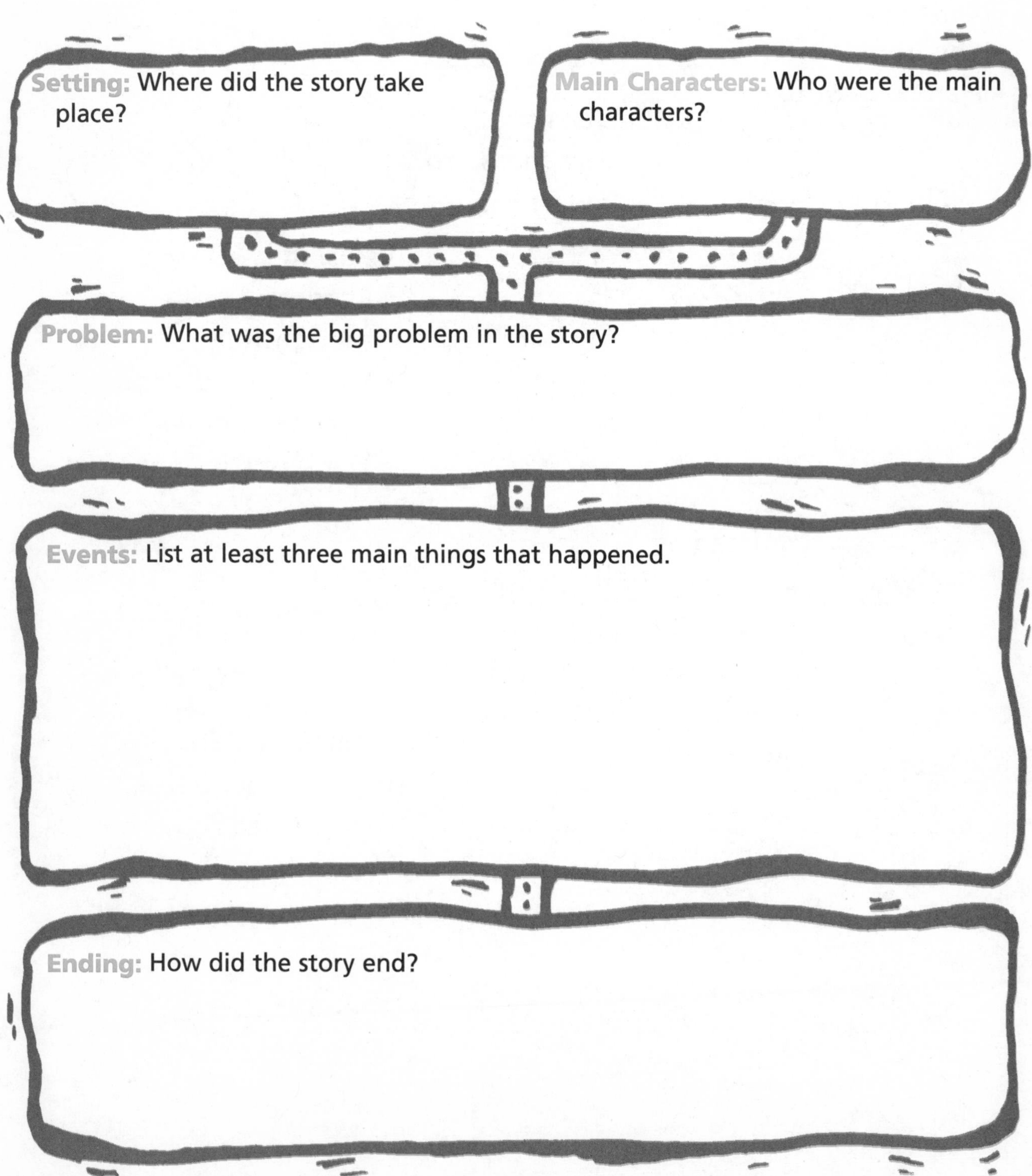

Name

The Writing Process

Prewriting
- Choose a topic.
- Plan your writing.

Drafting
- Write a first draft.
- Get your ideas down.
- Don't worry about mistakes.

Revising
- Read your draft thoughtfully.
- Make your ideas clear.
- Check the order.
- Think of strong words.

Proofreading
- Read your draft carefully again.
- Use proofreading marks.
- Correct spelling mistakes.
- Check capital letters and punctuation.

Publishing and Sharing
- Think of a good title.
- Make a clean copy and check it over.
- Find ways to share your writing.

Name

Off to a Good Start

Choosing a Topic List three or four choices to write about. Then put a check mark next to the one you will be writing about.

______________________ ______________________

______________________ ______________________

Plan Your Writing Write your topic in the top box. Put big ideas under your topic. Add details for each big idea. Keep adding ideas and details as you think of them. Use another piece of paper if you need more space.

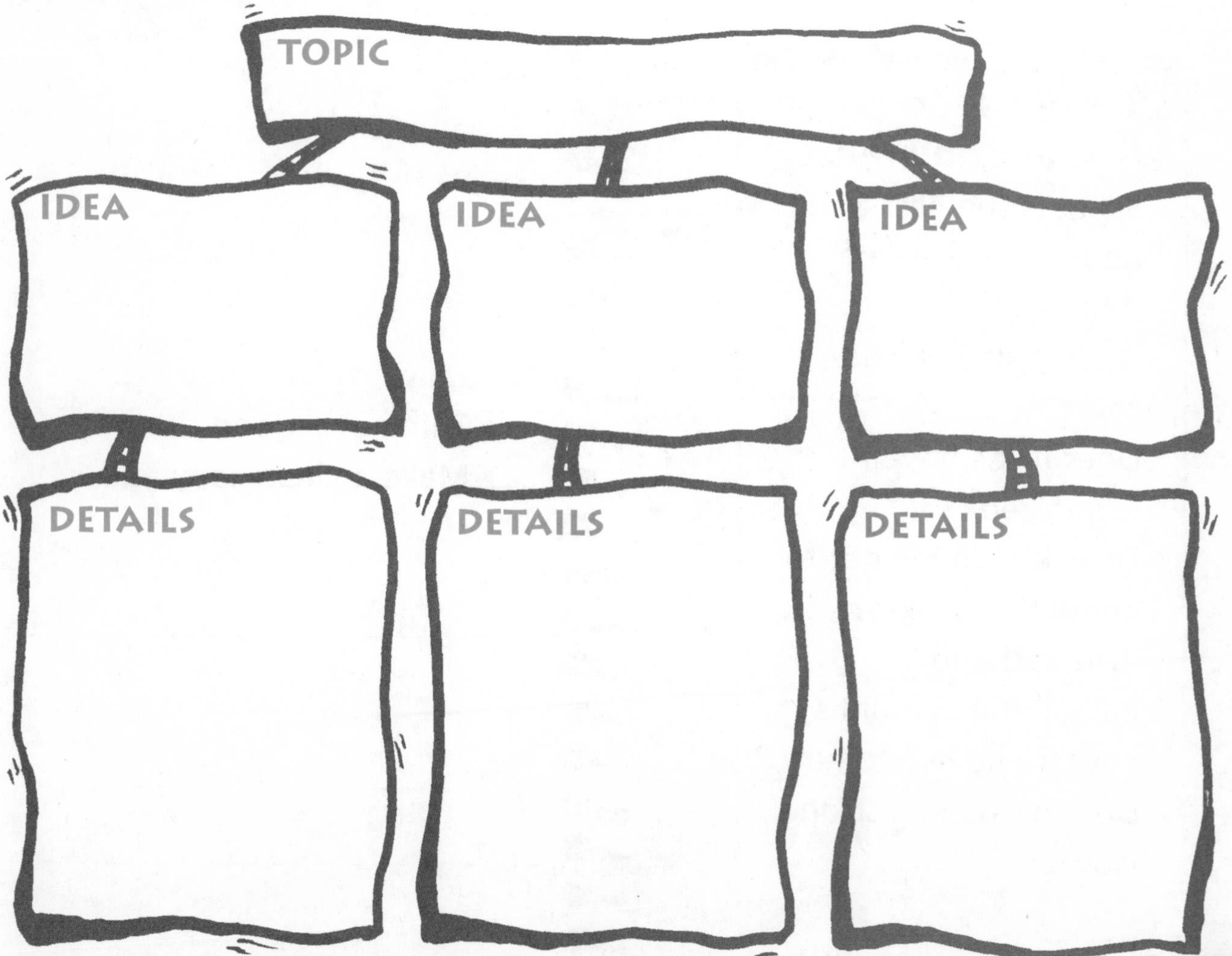

TOPIC

IDEA

IDEA

IDEA

DETAILS

DETAILS

DETAILS

Name

Revising Your Writing

Reread and revise your page of the class book. Use the Revising Checklist as a guide. Then have a writing conference with a classmate. Use the Questions for a Writing Conference to help your partner.

Revising Checklist

- ❑ Have I stated my main ideas clearly?
- ❑ Are there enough details and support?
- ❑ Is there anything I should leave out?
- ❑ Are my ideas in a good order?
- ❑ Have I used interesting words?

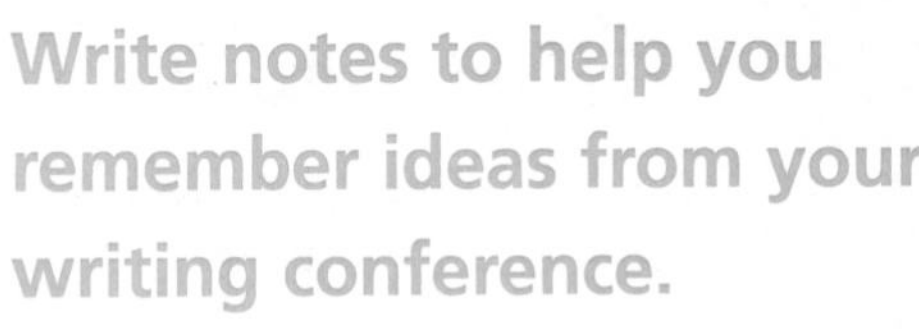

Questions for a Writing Conference

- What is the best thing about this piece of writing?
- Does it stay on the topic?
- Does it seem well organized?
- Does it help me get to know this person?
- What additional information would a new friend like to have?
- Does it end in a strong way?

Write notes to help you remember ideas from your writing conference.

My Notes

Name ______________________________

Oink, Oink, Oink

Tale with a Twist Create your own fractured folktale. First, complete items 1–6. Then use those answers to complete the story.

1. Name a funny animal.
   ____
2. Give the name of a faraway country.
   ____
3. Name a food that you hate.
   ____
4. Give a girl's name.
   ____
5. Name an action verb in the past tense.
   ____
6. Name an object you find inside.
   ____

Once upon a time, there was a ________ (1) family—a papa, a mama, and a baby. One day they went out for a walk in ________ (2) while their ________ (3) cooled.

Meanwhile, ________ (4) entered their house. She ate their ________ (3). She tried all of their beds and then ________ (5) on Baby's ________ (6).

When the ________ (1) family returned, they found ________ (4) still asleep. When she heard them, she ________ (5) again!

Name

Oink, Oink, Oink

In Oink, Oink, Oink, you will read three funny versions of "The Three Little Pigs." After you read each story, fill in this chart.

	The Three Little Wolves and the Big Bad Pig	The Three Little Javelinas	The Three Little Hawaiian Pigs and the Magic Shark
Setting			
Main Characters			
Building Materials			
Main Events			
Ending			

Name

Get the Message?

Detective Fox found these messages on his telephone answering machine. Choose a word from the box to complete each message.

crumbled	grunted
prowling	trembling

Message #1

From: The Three Bears

We think someone has been ________________ around our house. The porridge is gone, and we found bits of bread ________________ all over the floor. We're afraid to look in the bedroom. Please come at once!

Message #2

From: Little Red Riding Hood

I'm at Grandmother's house. I think there's a wolf in her bed, and I'm ________________ with fear. Hurry! I'm really scared!

Message #3

From: Mother Pig

My youngest son called yesterday. His voice sounded strange. He ________________ something about a huffing and a puffing at his door. Please check it out. His house is the brick one.

Name ______________________________

What a Week!

The Big Bad Pig wrote a letter to his brother. Complete the letter to tell what happened in the story.

Dear Hammond,

I had an incredible week. It began when I came upon a ______________________ built by these three wolves. At first I tried ______________________, but then I decided to use a sledgehammer to ______________________. Soon after, they built a house of ______________________. It was a bit more work, but my ______________________ smashed that house down. Then they collected ______________________ ______________________ and built their strongest house. I needed ______________________ to demolish that one. Their last house was the best, though. It was made of sweet-smelling ______________________. I decided this is where I'd love to live! So now I play games like ______________________ ______________________ with my furry friends. Come visit sometime!

Sincerely,

____

Name

Winter Dance

Read the fable. Then complete the chart.

One winter day, some ants were hard at work in a field. A grasshopper came along and asked if the ants could give him a few grains of corn. "Please," said the grasshopper, "for I am starving."

"What did you do all last summer while we gathered food?" the ants asked.

The grasshopper replied, "I was busy singing."

"Then you can dance all winter," said the ants.

Setting	
Characters	
Problem	
Events	
Ending	

Name

Home Repairs

Help the three little wolves rebuild the house. Make each sentence fragment into a complete sentence. Write the sentence on a brick.

built a wall

huffed and puffed

called the police

one of my brothers

the big bad pig

1

2

3

4

5

Name

What a Gift

The three little wolves bought their new friend the pig a T-shirt. Solve the puzzle to find out what was printed on the shirt.

Each word has a base word. Write the base word. Then write each numbered letter on the T-shirt.

precooked ___ ___ ___ ___ (8, 14)

mislead ___ ___ ___ ___ (4, 9)

remover ___ ___ ___ ___ (7)

unfolded ___ ___ ___ ___ (2, 13)

enjoy ___ ___ ___ (1)

agreement ___ ___ ___ ___ ___ (6, 11)

unhappiness ___ ___ ___ ___ ___ (5)

weekly ___ ___ ___ ___ (15)

lived ___ ___ ___ ___ (12)

selfish ___ ___ ___ ___ (3, 10)

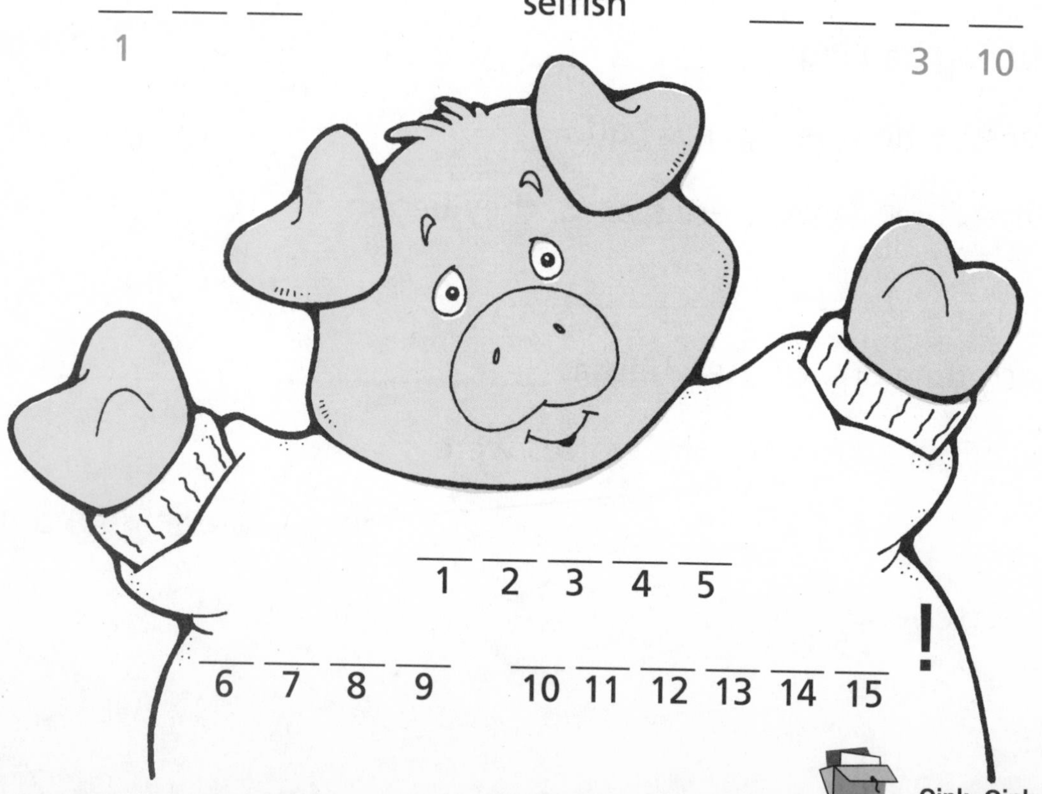

Name

A Bad Temper

The Big Good Pig is feeling like a Big Bad Pig again because he is having trouble with the sentences. Help him feel good by completing each sentence with the better of the two words in parentheses.

1. The three little wolves looked soft and ______________ (cuddly, messy).
2. In order to sneak up on the wolves, the Big Bad Pig came ______________ (running, prowling) through the trees.
3. The Big Bad Pig ______________ (grunted, swayed) because he was big and bad.
4. When the wolves were scared, they began ______________ (trembling, playing).
5. Each time one of their houses ______________ (crumbled, fetched), the wolves were ______________ (frightened, determined) to build a better one.

Name

Flower Power

Short Vowels Each Spelling Word has a short vowel sound. A short vowel sound is usually spelled ***a, e, i, o,*** or ***u*** and is followed by a consonant sound.

short *a*	/ă/	ask	short *o*	/ŏ/	lock
short *e*	/ĕ/	next	short *u*	/ŭ/	shut
short *i*	/ĭ/	mix			

Spelling Words

1. **ask**
2. **next**
3. **mix**
4. **smell**
5. **black**
6. **shut**
7. **lock**
8. **truck**

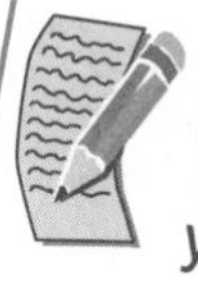

My Study List
What other words do you need to study for spelling? Add them to My Study List for The Three Little Wolves and the Big, Bad Pig in the back of this book.

Write each Spelling Word next to the flower that has the matching vowel sound.

/ă/
1 ______
2 ______

/ĕ/
3 ______
4 ______

/ĭ/
5 ______

/ŏ/
6 ______

/ŭ/
7 ______
8 ______

Name

Spelling Spree

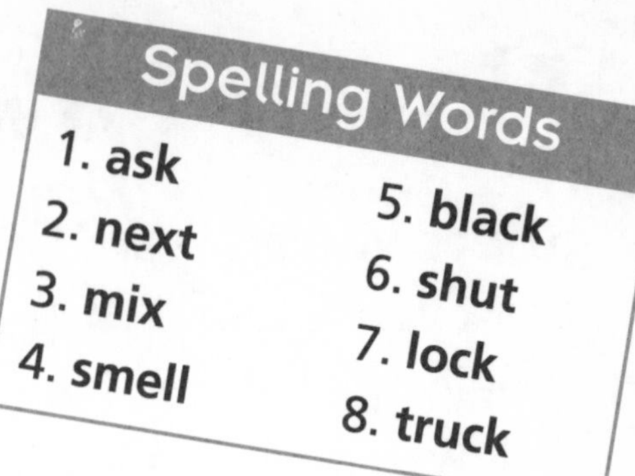

Proofreading Find and circle four misspelled Spelling Words in this song. Then write each word correctly.

The Piggy Jig

Whenever the sky is rainy and blak,
I locke all my cares away.
Then I shut my eyes and smel the flowers,
And find the nixt mud hole for play!

1. ______
2. ______
3. ______
4. ______

Riddles Write a Spelling Word to answer each riddle.

5. If you have a question, you do this. What is this? ______
6. Before you bake a cake, you do this. What is this? ______
7. This opens with a key. What is this? ______
8. This has four wheels. What is this? ______
9. Your nose can do this for you. What is this? ______
10. Your eyes do this when you fall asleep. What is this? ______

Build It Up Imagine that you are going to build something. On a separate paper, write step-by-step directions for how to do it. Use Spelling Words from the list.

Name

Piece It Together

Subjects and Predicates

Color red each puzzle piece that has a subject. Color blue each puzzle piece that has a predicate. Then cut out and match the puzzle pieces to make sentences.

SUBJECT	PREDICATE
The wolf	laid the bricks.

this story

the four animals

many famous stories

is a very old one

scares some small children

it

live happily ever after

read the story to children

teachers

are about animals

On another piece of paper, write the sentences. Begin each sentence with a capital letter. End each sentence with a period.

PASTE

Name

Picture Perfect

Subjects and Predicates The little wolves took pictures of their homes. Write a sentence about each one. Write the subject in the Subject box. Write the predicate in the Predicate box.

Subject	Predicate

Name

Way to Go

Two javelinas received secret directions from their sister. To confuse Coyote, she used the underlined definitions in her directions rather than the words themselves. Fill in the blanks with the correct words.

Walk a mile into our wonderful sunny, sandy land (______________). Keep an eye out for you-know-who! If he does sneak up behind you, huff and puff to make a blast of spinning air (______________) that will knock him right off his paws! Then RUN! Turn right at the plant with the sharp needles (______________). Walk just a little farther. Look for some yellow flowers. It may be hard to see them since those little rolling bushes (______________) are always getting in the way. I'll be in my cozy mud brick (______________) house waiting.

WARNING: I heard there's a chance of a sand and dirt twister (______________). Come prepared just in case!

Name ______________________

According to Coyote

If Coyote could talk, how would he tell the story? Complete Coyote's statements to retell *The Three Little Javelinas*.

1. The first javelina built a ______________________ ____________. I ____________ ______________________, but he got away!

2. The second javelina tried using ______________________ ______________________ ____________. I knocked them down, but he and his brother ran away!

3. I pretended to be ______________________ ______________________ to get into the third javelina's house. When that failed, I tried ______________________ ______________________ ____________.

4. Ouch! The three javelinas surprised me by ______________________ ______________________ ____________. I'll never forget it!

Name

Like It or Not

How does the desert setting of *The Three Little Javelinas* compare and contrast with where you live? Think about the weather, the land, the plants, and the animals.

Write your responses in the Venn diagram. Remember that similar things in both settings go in the middle.

Desert

Both Settings

My Home Region

Name

Writing a Book Report

Use this form as a guide for writing a book report. Jot down all your information and ideas. Then write your book report on another piece of paper.

Title ______________________________

Author ______________________________

Main Characters ______________________________

____

Where the Story Takes Place ______________________________

____

Story Events or Main Idea ______________________________

____

____

____

____

Your Opinion of the Book ______________________________

____

____

____

____

____

Name

Which Ending?

Coyote is clever, but he can't read the words on the chalkboard. Fill in the chart to help him to see that each word is made from a base word plus the ending -*ed* or -*ing*.

	Base Word	-ed or -ing
scaring	scare	ing
flipped	flip	ed
1. sneaking		
2. thanked		
3. chased		
4. topping		
5. piling		
6. jogged		
7. giggling		
8. mixed		
9. winning		
10. dared		

Name

Word Families

Put the words in the correct category. Some words may go in more than one category. Then add words of your own.

desert	dust storm	whirlwind	tumbleweeds
cactus	adobe	saguaro	palo verde

Name

Home Sweet Home

Spelling Words
1. nose
2. these
3. shade
4. use
5. mice
6. smoke
7. snake
8. ripe

My Study List
What other words do you need to study for spelling? Add them to My Study List for *The Three Little Javelinas* in the back of this book.

Vowel-Consonant-*e* Each Spelling Word has a long vowel sound spelled with the vowel-consonant-**e** pattern.

long *a* /ā/ shade
long *e* /ē/ these
long *i* /ī/ mice
long *o* /ō/ nose
long *u* /yōō/ use

Write the Spelling Word that matches the vowel-consonant-e pattern on each house.

/ā/
a-consonant-*e*
1 ____________
2 ____________

/ē/
e-consonant-*e*
3 ____________

/ī/
i-consonant-*e*
4 ____________
5 ____________

/ō/
o-consonant-*e*
6 ____________
7 ____________

/ū/
u-consonant-*e*
8 ____________

Name

Spelling Spree

Spelling Words

1. nose
2. these
3. shade
4. use
5. mice
6. smoke
7. snake
8. ripe

Rhyme Time Write the Spelling Word that rhymes with the underlined word.

1. The desert is hot. I'd love to trade this sunny spot for some cool, dark ________.
2. "Oh!" cried the child, though the toy was fake. It wiggled and slid like a long, black ________.
3. Ms. Glade sniffed the air and began to choke. Wherever there's fire, there's usually ________.
4. Ramon ate the pear without a gripe because fruit is so tasty whenever it's ________.

Proofreading Find and circle four misspelled Spelling Words in Coyote's diary. Then write each word correctly.

April 2
Poor me! I burned my noes, and I can't smell a thing! I can't run thees days either because I tried to uze my paws to put out the fire. Today, I'm starting a new diet! I'm just sitting here under a cactus, nibbling its ripe fruit, and dreaming about tasty mise!

5. ________ 7. ________
6. ________ 8. ________

See a Tree The javelinas lived among cactus and palo verde trees. On a separate piece of paper, describe a plant or tree where you live. Use Spelling Words from the list.

Name

Run-on Riddles

Run-on This is the largest desert plant its fruit is red.

This is the largest desert plant. Its fruit is red.

Correcting Run-on Sentences

Read each run-on sentence. Then write the two sentences correctly. Last, answer the riddles!

ANSWERS?

1. She built a strong house it had a tin roof.

WHO WAS SHE?

2. He could make himself small he knew many tricks.

WHO WAS HE?

3. He fell down his house fell down, too.

WHO WAS HE?

4. Its fire did the trick Coyote was gone for good.

WHAT WAS IT?

5. They are made of mud people build with them.

WHAT ARE THEY?

Name

It's a Secret!

Correcting Run-on Sentences Find the secret word. First, write the two sentences in each run-on sentence. Write the first letter of each sentence in the box.

1. Two houses were very weak unsafe houses are dangerous.

☐ ______________________________

☐ ______________________________

2. Mud bricks make a good house bricks last a long time.

☐ ______________________________

☐ ______________________________

3. Little stick houses give shade even these houses can be strong.

☐ ______________________________

☐ ______________________________

4. Walls can be made of weeds every weed house needs support.

☐ ______________________________

☐ ______________________________

5. Each house was different desert houses are special

☐ ______________________________

☐ ______________________________

Now write all the first letters in order to find the secret word!

☐☐☐☐☐☐☐☐☐☐

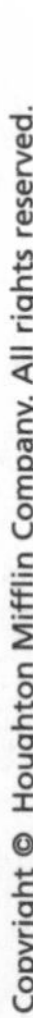

Name

Word Webs

Complete each word web.
Add one or two words from the box.

plot	scheme	craving
anxiously	furious	pangs

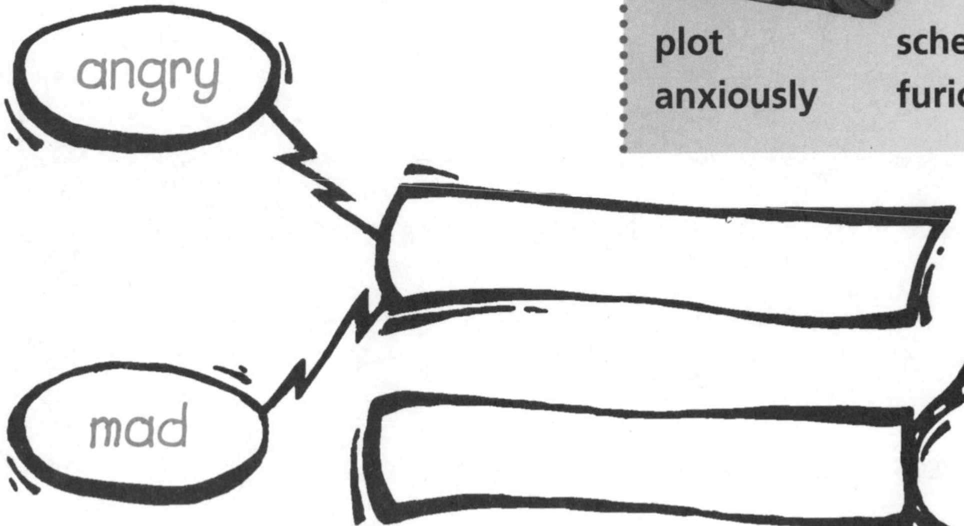

angry

mad

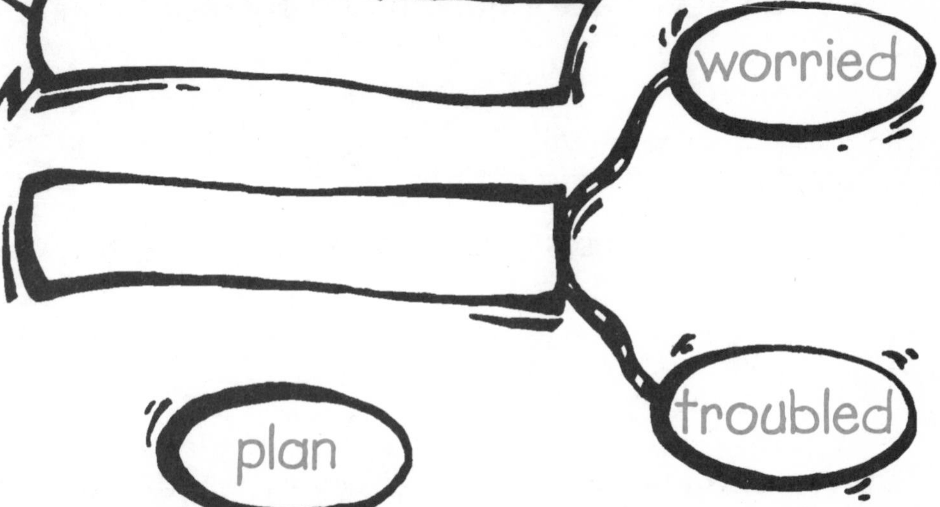

worried

troubled

plan

hunger

Name

Hawaiian Style

Here are the Hawaiian words for *yes* and *no*.

Read each sentence. If it tells something that happened in the story, write **ae**. If it does not, write **aole**.

_______ 1 The pigs' parents told them to watch out for wolves.

_______ 2 The first pig built a house of pili grass.

_______ 3 The second pig built a house of seashells.

_______ 4 The third pig built a house of lava rock.

_______ 5 All three little pigs liked to fish.

_______ 6 One day the pigs caught a magic shark.

_______ 7 The shark blew down two of the pigs' houses.

_______ 8 The shark blew himself out of air at the third pig's house.

_______ 9 The pigs rolled the shark up and dumped him in the ocean.

_______ 10 The third pig helped his brothers build lava rock houses.

Name

Is It Real?

Read the fable. Then write which parts are real and which are fantasy.

The Pig and the Sheep

One day a shepherd found a pig in his sheep pasture. He quickly caught the pig and tucked it under his arm. "I wonder what the butcher will give me for this fat little porker," he said as he started for town.

Now the pig started to squeal its head off — even though the shepherd wasn't really hurting it.

This puzzled the sheep, who followed and asked, "Why ever are you squealing so? *We* don't make such a fuss when he carries one of us off!"

Tearfully, the pig responded, "All he wants is your wool. But he wants my bacon!"

Moral: It's easy to be brave when your life is not in danger.

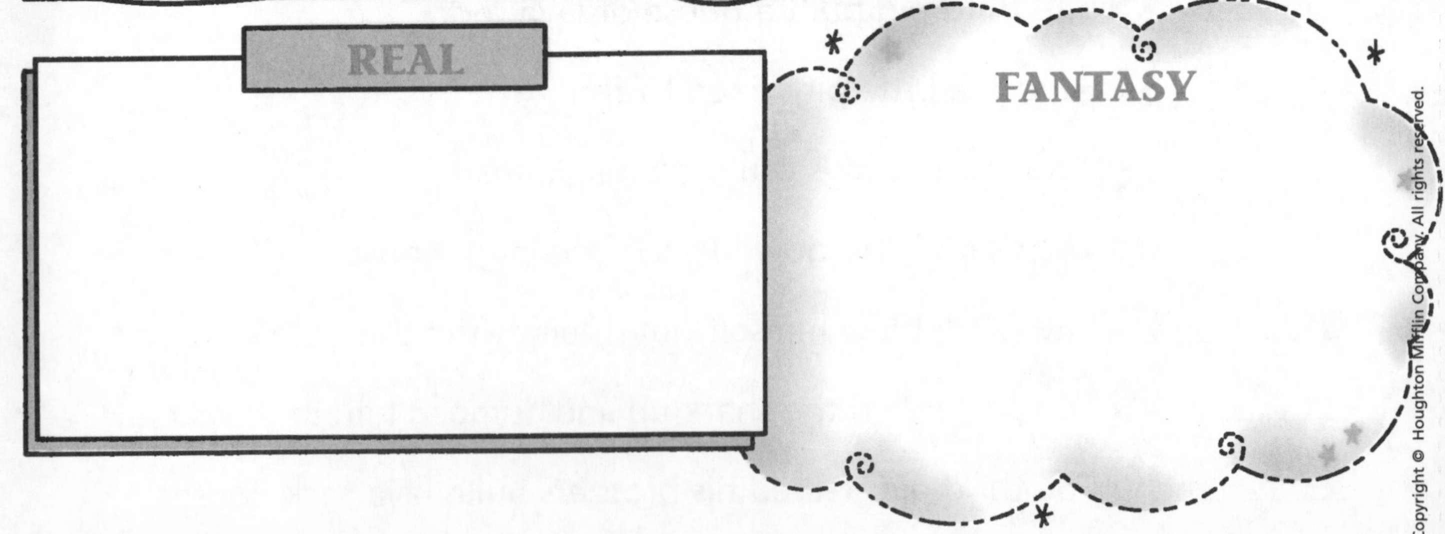

Name

Two to One

This story is about the three little pigs and the magic shark. Look for five sentences that could be combined. Write them as compound sentences.

Three Little Heroes

This week, three little pigs have become heroes! They took care of a pesky shark. The shark came into their yard. The pigs ran inside to hide. One pig began closing windows. Another locked the front door. The shark started knocking with his big fin. He was very hungry. The pigs were very scared. The angry shark began to huff and puff. The house shook. Finally, the shark ran out of air. He fell in a heap. The pigs took him off to the dump. The shark won't be bothering them anymore!

1 ________________________________

2 ________________________________

3 ________________________________

4 ________________________________

5 ________________________________

Name

Figure It Out

Use context clues to figure out the meaning of each underlined word. Circle the clues in the sentence. Then write the meaning.

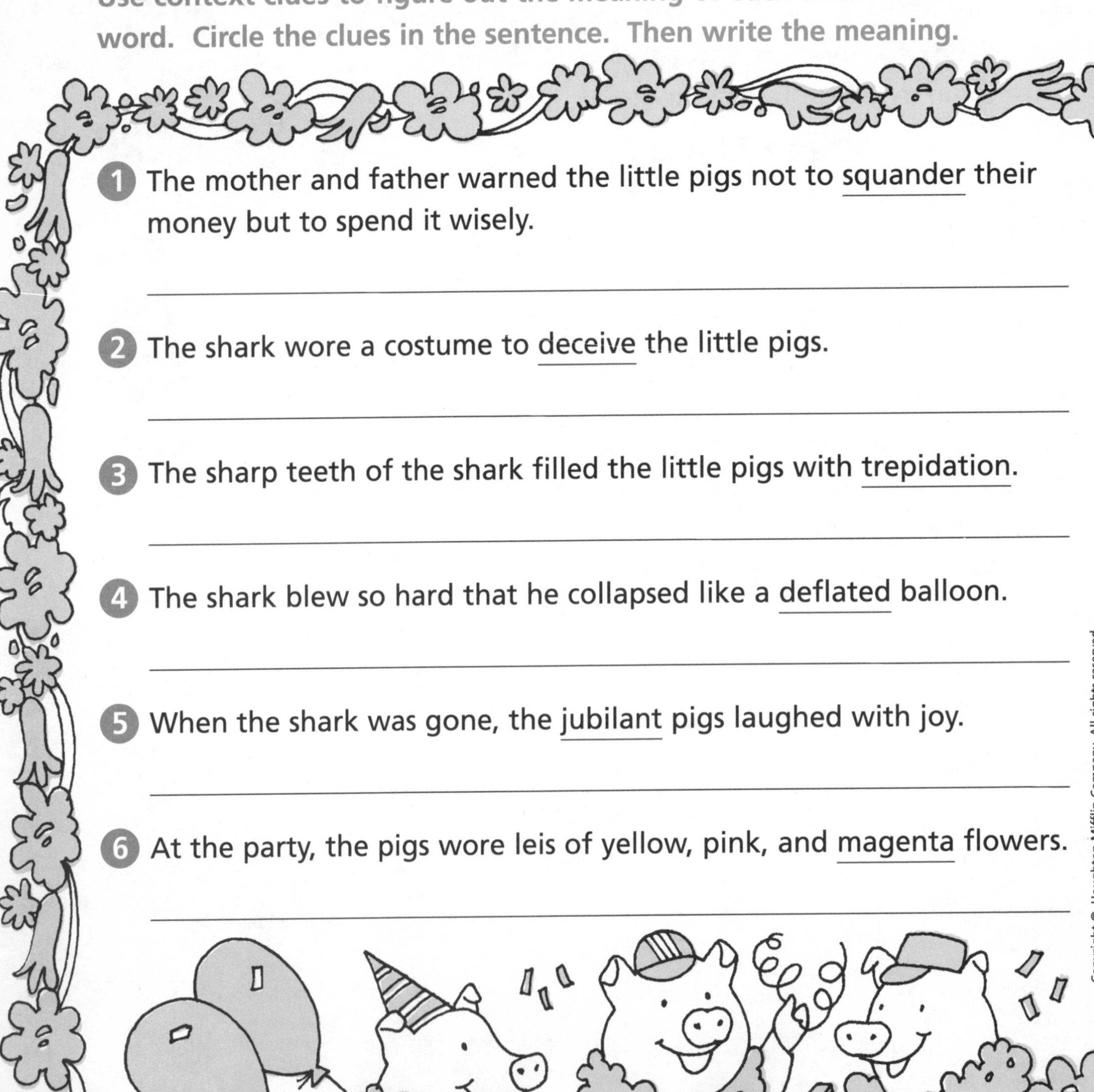

1. The mother and father warned the little pigs not to squander their money but to spend it wisely.

2. The shark wore a costume to deceive the little pigs.

3. The sharp teeth of the shark filled the little pigs with trepidation.

4. The shark blew so hard that he collapsed like a deflated balloon.

5. When the shark was gone, the jubilant pigs laughed with joy.

6. At the party, the pigs wore leis of yellow, pink, and magenta flowers.

Name

It's Puzzling!

Find the words from the box in the word search. Words can go across, up, down, or diagonally. When you have found all the words, answer the questions.

craving	furious
anxiously	sorrow
plot	sturdy
scheme	roared
pangs	firm

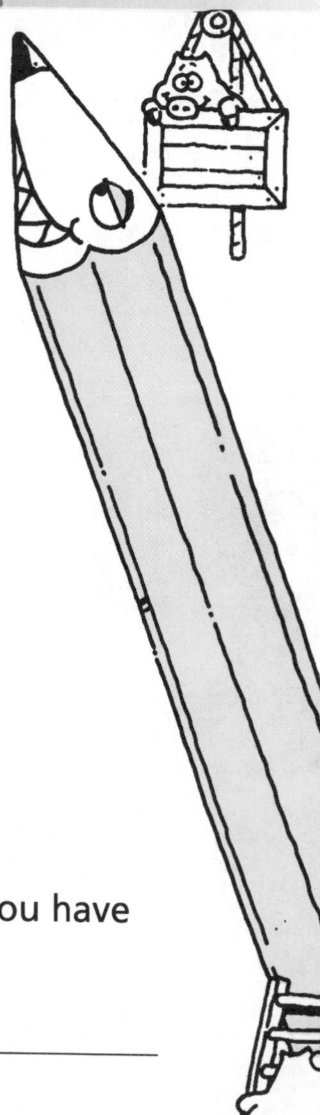

1. When you have hunger **pangs**, for what do you have a **craving**?

____

____

2. What do people do when they **plot** and **scheme**?

____

____

Name

Sea Sights

Long *a* and Long *e* Some Spelling Words have the |ā| sound spelled with the pattern ***ai*** or ***ay.***

|ā| tail play

The other Spelling Words have the |ē| sound spelled with the pattern ***ea*** or ***ee.***

|ē| beach three

Spelling Words

1. **three**
2. **tail**
3. **beach**
4. **play**
5. **deep**
6. **away**
7. **please**
8. **chain**

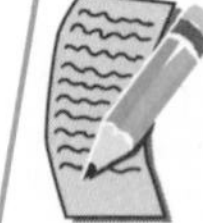

My Study List
What other words do you need to study for spelling? Add them to My Study List for *The Three Little Hawaiian Pigs and the Magic Shark* in the back of this book.

Write the Spelling Words that match the pattern next to each sea creature.

|ā| → ai

|ā| → ay

1. ____________
2. ____________

5. ____________
6. ____________

|ē| → ea

|ē| → ee

3. ____________
4. ____________

7. ____________
8. ____________

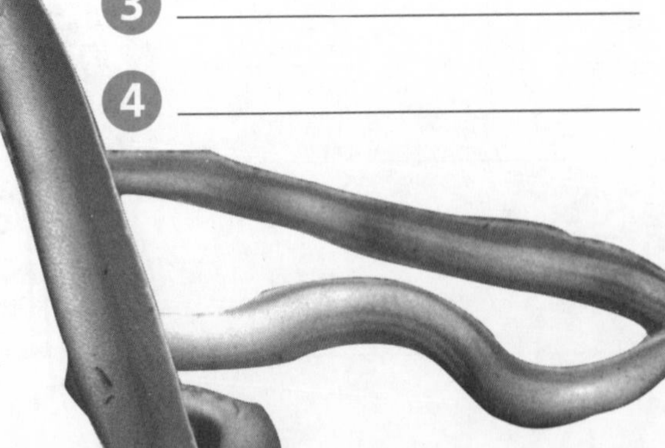

Name

Spelling Spree

Spelling Words

1. three
2. tail
3. beach
4. play
5. deep
6. away
7. please
8. chain

Hink Pinks Write the Spelling Word that fits the clue and rhymes with the given word.

Example:

a daring rescue — a brave <u>save</u>

1. twenty-four hours of games — a ________ day
2. an army car stuck in a huge hole — a ________ jeep
3. metal links that are not fancy — a plain ________
4. a white bird's end feathers — a pale ________

Proofreading Find and circle four misspelled Spelling Words in this invitation. Then write each word correctly.

Dear Friend,

It would pleaze us to have you come to our beech party next Sunday. We will meet at threa o'clock at our house. We will swim, play games, and eat shave ice. Put awai all your work. Come have fun in the sun!

Aloha,

The Three Hawaiian Pigs

5. ________
6. ________
7. ________
8. ________

Party Time On a separate piece of paper, write an invitation to a party. Tell where and when it will be. Use Spelling Words from the list.

Name

Asking or Telling

Kinds of Sentences Jamie interviewed the third little pig. Three questions and answers are given below. Write each question and its answer on a notepad. Add the correct end marks.

How long did you work on your house	I saw him in the water
Where did you first see the shark	I was terrified
I worked for a whole month	Were you afraid

Q. ____________________

A. ____________________

Q. ____________________

A. ____________________

Q. ____________________

A. ____________________

Extra! Interview the shark! Write your questions and his answers on another sheet of paper. Write at least two questions and two statements.

Name

What Kind?

Kinds of Sentences Help the Hawaiian pigs make some signs for the beach. Each sentence is a command or an exclamation. Add the correct end mark. Then write **command** or **exclamation** to show what kind of sentence it is.

1. Rent a fishing boat

   ______

2. Walk this way to the beach

   ______

3. Sharks swim here

   ______

4. That is a shark

   ______

5. Give me your hand

   ______

6. How hot it is

   ______

Extra! Write a command and an exclamation of your own. Use correct end marks. Label each sentence.

7. ______ ______

8. ______ ______

Name

Terrific Topics

Story Ideas Do any of these ideas spark an idea for your story?

- a strange friendship between a wolf and a pig
- a trip in a time machine
- taking a rocket to Jupiter
- finding a lost puppy
- an amazing amusement park
- a talking ant

My Story Ideas

Write five ideas for your own story here.

____

____

____

____

____

Can I picture the characters and setting clearly?

Think about each idea you wrote. Then ask yourself the three questions.

Do I have enough ideas for the beginning, middle, and end?

Do I really want to write about this idea?

Name

A Good Start

Write and draw details about your story.
Use another piece of paper if you need more space.

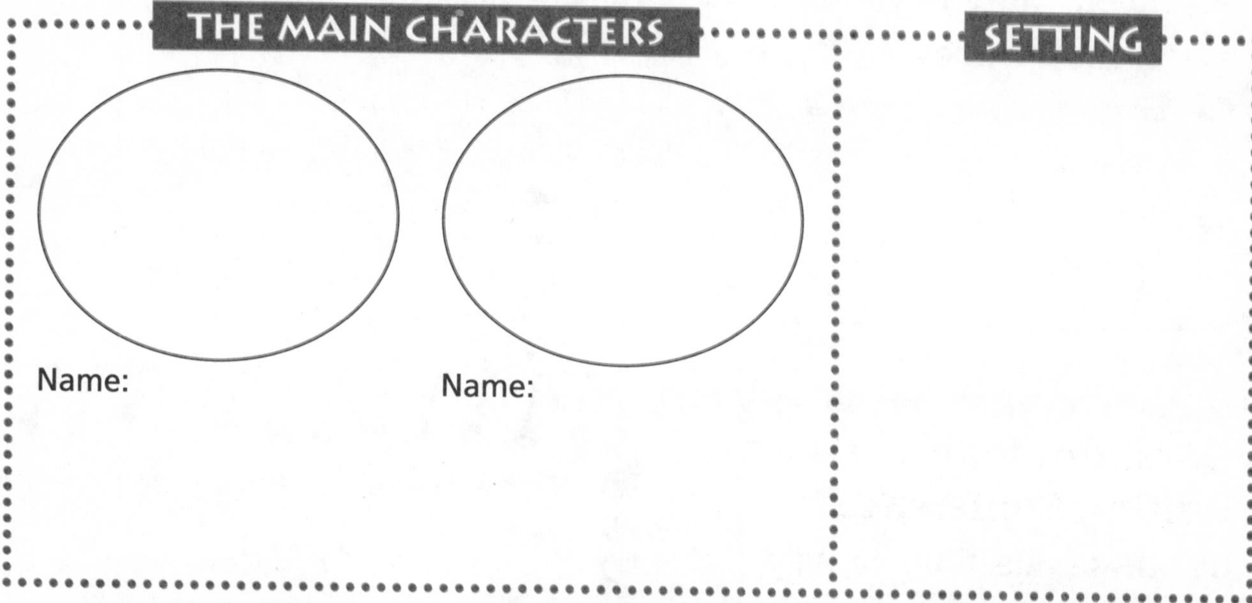

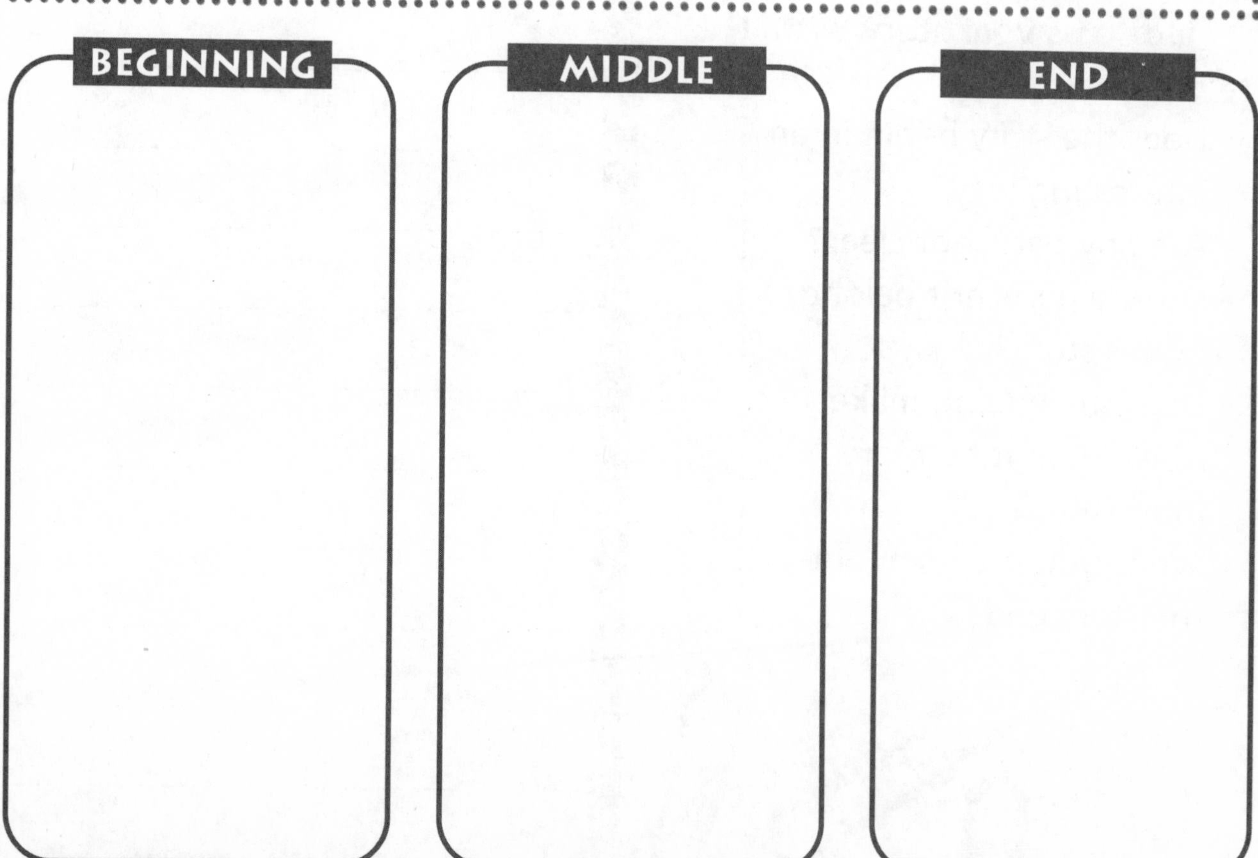

Name

Take Another Look

Revising Checklist

Read your story to yourself. Ask yourself these questions and make changes.

- ❑ Does it have a beginning, a middle, and an end?
- ❑ Does it tell about one problem or situation?
- ❑ Did I use dialogue?
- ❑ Could my readers picture the characters and the events?

Questions for a Writing Conference

Use these questions to help you discuss your story with a classmate.

- Does the story begin in an interesting way?
- Are any parts not clear?
- Do any parts not belong in this story?
- Does the ending make sense? Can it be more interesting?
- What other ways might the story end?

Write notes to remember ideas.

My Notes

Name ....

New Pigs on the Block

Read this summary of "The Three Little Pigs."

Three pigs built houses of straw, sticks, and bricks. A wolf blew down the straw and the stick houses and ate the two pigs. The wolf couldn't blow down the brick house, so he jumped down the chimney and fell into a pot of soup on the fire. Then the third pig ate the wolf.

Invent your own version of "The Three Little Pigs." Use the chart to help you. Check whether each part of your story is alike or different from "The Three Little Pigs."

	Alike	Different
Characters		
Problem		
Events 1. 2. 3.		
Ending		

On a strip of paper, draw your story scenes in order. Use your story strip to tell your version of "The Three Little Pigs."

Checklist Use this list to check your work.

- ☐ My story retells "The Three Little Pigs" in a new way.
- ☐ My story has characters, a problem, events, and an ending.
- ☐ I can use my story strip to tell my story.
- ☐ I can compare my story to "The Three Little Pigs."

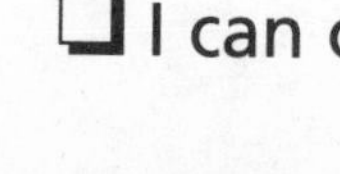

Name

Community Ties

Read the flyer and respond to the request for help.

SAVE YOUR COMMUNITY CENTER

We need your help to repair the community center. You can help by raising money or by hammering a nail. Please let us know the different ways you can help us rebuild your community center.

YOU CAN HELP TOO!

1.
2.
3.
4.
5.

Please return this flyer to:

Your Community Leader
100234 Community St.
Your Community, Your State 01234

Name

Community Ties

How did being part of the community help these people?

A Fruit & Vegetable Man

Ruby

Sun Ho

Family Pictures/Cuadros de familia

Carmen Lomas Garza

Her Family

When Jo Louis Won the Title

John Henry

Jo Louis

How can *you* be a helpful community tie?

Name

Play with Your Food

Follow the directions to create your own market. You may want to work with a partner.

1. Cut out all the items on this page.
2. Arrange the fruit in the shape of a **triangle**.
3. Now arrange the fruit in the shape of a **diamond**.
4. Next, arrange the fruit in the shape of a **pyramid**.
5. Then arrange the fruit in **designs** of your choice.
6. Use the vegetable to add an **accent** to your designs.
7. Finally, make a sign for your **market**.

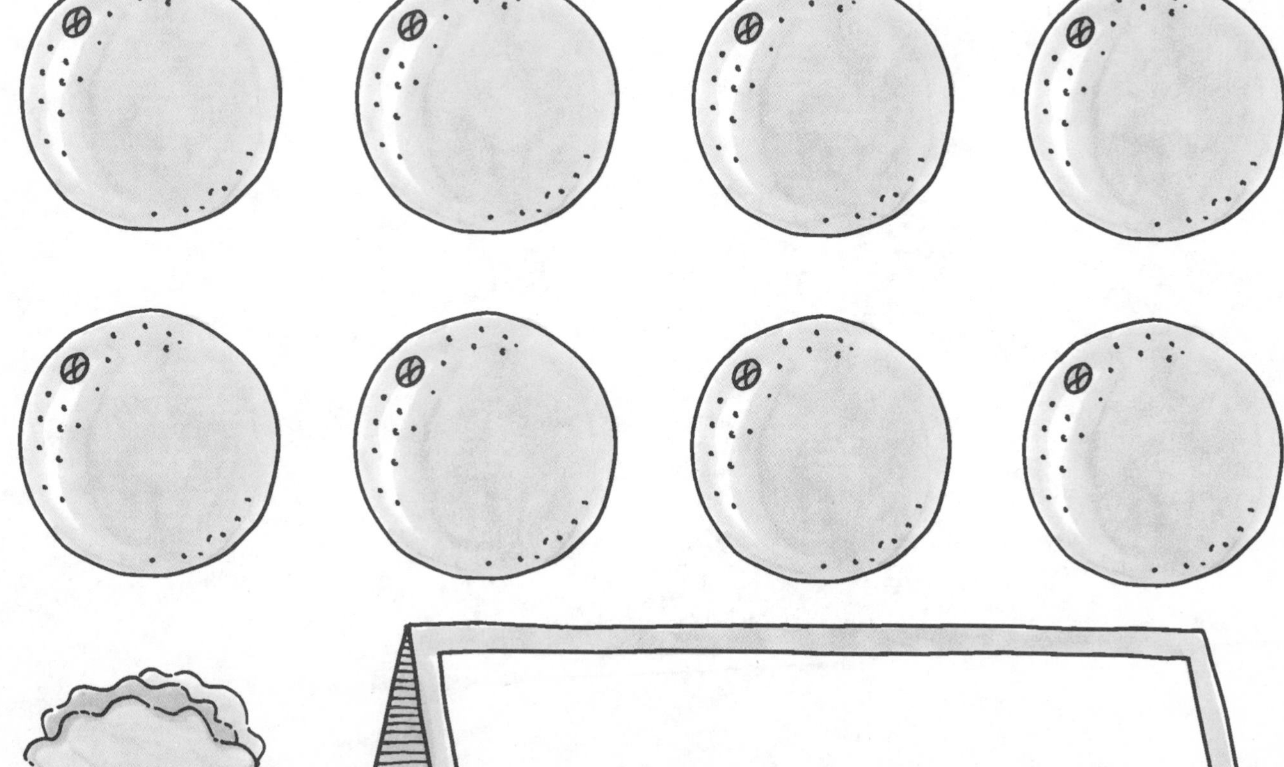

Name ______________________________

The Ruby and Sun Ho Story

Tell the story by filling in the chart.

Main Characters	
Setting	
Problem	
Events	
Ending	

Name

Details, Details!

Look at the pictures. Write details from the story that tell what is going on in each picture.

1

2

3

Name

Writing an Essay

Think about the things that make you feel proud. Write down some of your ideas.

Choose one idea that you might like to write about and circle it. Then write a sentence that expresses your feelings. Your sentence should answer this question: What makes me feel proud?

Now list three or four examples of how this thing makes you feel proud.

Name

Market Day

Read about Ruby on the canopy. Find the plural nouns in the paragraph and write them on the base of the cart.

Ruby gets up at dawn every morning. He has to go to market to choose fruits and vegetables for his store. Ruby sniffs lemons, squeezes tomatoes, and wrinkles up his eyes to squint at the apples. He's on the lookout for bruises, worms, or rotten spots—only the finest for his customers back at the store! Ruby always teases his way to better prices while his purchases are weighed on the scale. Finally, he pays and makes his way back to his store in the city.

1. __________
2. __________
3. __________
4. __________
5. __________
6. __________
7. __________
8. __________
9. __________
10. __________
11. __________
12. __________

Name

A Helpful Reminder

Ruby wanted to leave Sun Ho a list of things to do, but he forgot to finish the list. Use the words in the box and your own words to finish the list.

triangles
fresh
diamonds
designs
ripe
accent
pyramids

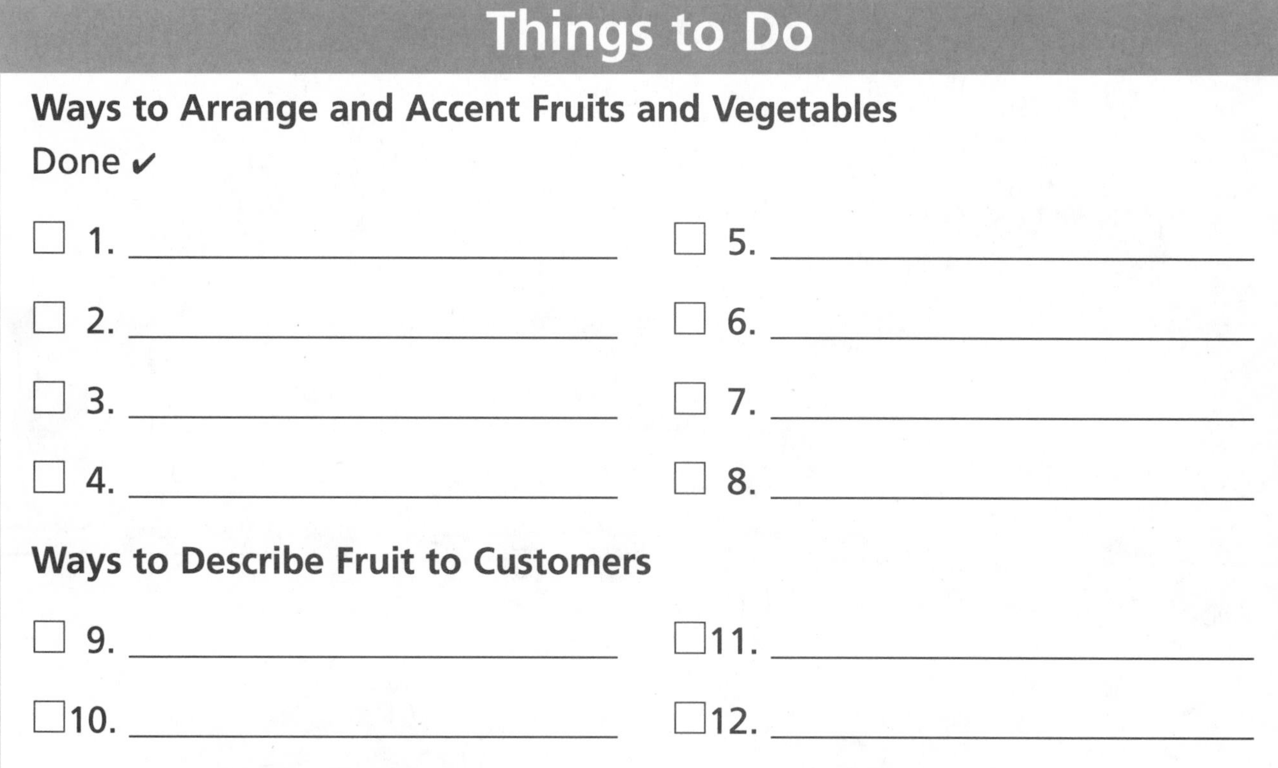

Things to Do

Ways to Arrange and Accent Fruits and Vegetables

Done ✔

☐ 1. ______________ ☐ 5. ______________

☐ 2. ______________ ☐ 6. ______________

☐ 3. ______________ ☐ 7. ______________

☐ 4. ______________ ☐ 8. ______________

Ways to Describe Fruit to Customers

☐ 9. ______________ ☐ 11. ______________

☐ 10. ______________ ☐ 12. ______________

Name

Fruit Stand

Long *i* and Long *o* Some Spelling Words have the |ī| sound spelled with the pattern ***igh*** or ***ie***.

|ī| right tie

The other Spelling Words have the |ō| sound spelled with the pattern ***oa*** or ***ow***.

|ō| soap own

Spelling Words

1. **own**
2. **right**
3. **row**
4. **might**
5. **tie**
6. **soap**
7. **pie**
8. **float**

My Study List
What other words do you need to study for spelling? Add them to My Study List for *A Fruit & Vegetable Man* in the back of this book.

Help Ruby sort fruit. Write the Spelling Words that match the pattern with each kind of fruit.

|ī| **igh**

1 ____________________

2 ____________________

|ī| **ie**

5 ____________________

6 ____________________

|ō| **oa**

3 ____________________

4 ____________________

|ō| **ow**

7 ____________________

8 ____________________

Name

Spelling Spree

Spelling Words

1. own
2. right
3. row
4. might
5. tie
6. soap
7. pie
8. float

Crossword Cart Fill the shopping cart. Write the Spelling Word that fits each clue.

Across

2. may

5. what boats do

6. a dessert that may be filled with fruit

Down

1. true or correct

3. to knot laces together

4. _____ and water

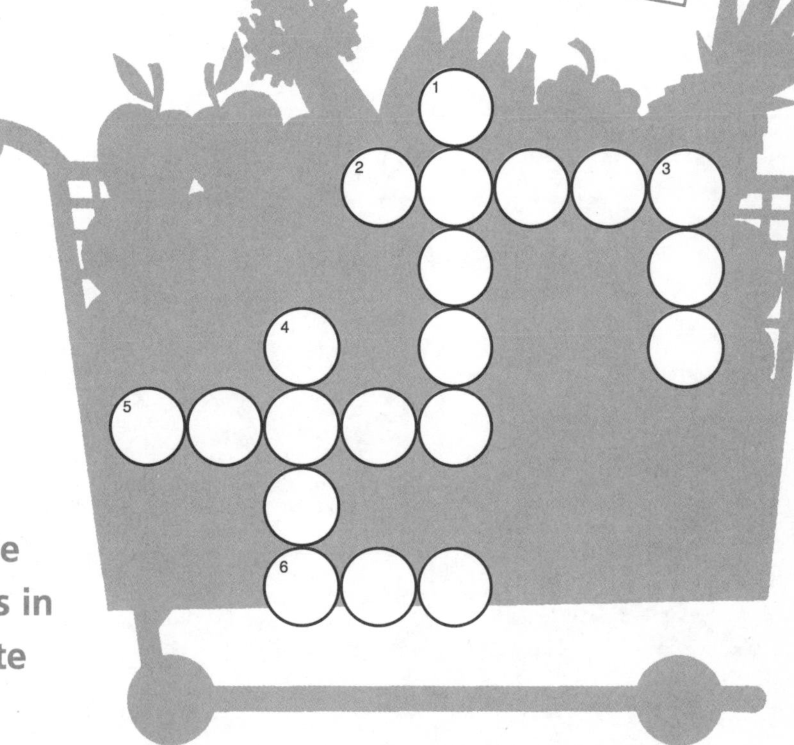

Proofreading Find and circle four misspelled Spelling Words in this announcement. Then write each word correctly.

Come to the Fruit Mart's first baking class! We use our oan fruit to make your favorite pye! Choose from any rowe of apples, peaches, or pears. Learn the rite way to make a crust. Then take home what you make. You might be surprised at how good it is!

 ________  ________  ________  ________

Fresh Picks What is your favorite fruit or vegetable? On a separate piece of paper, describe your choice and tell why you like it. Use Spelling Words from the list.

Name ....

Boxes of Carrots

PEOPLE

PLACES

THINGS

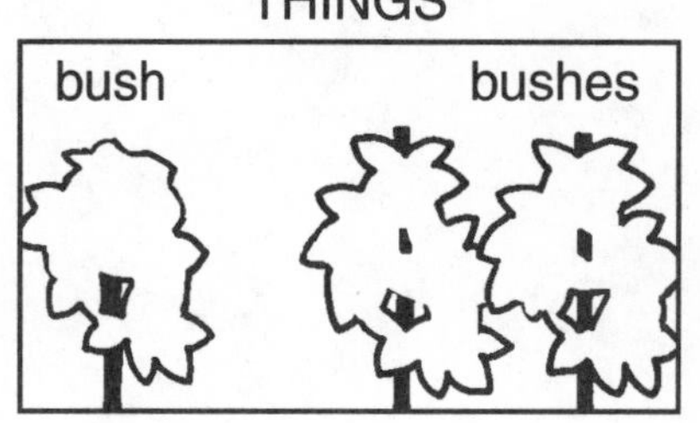

Nouns Circle the nouns and write each one in a carrot.

1. The old man was like an artist.
2. Sometimes his feet hurt.
3. The children loved the store.
4. Some berries were piled in boxes.
5. The bunches of carrots lay on a shelf.

Draw two boxes on a different piece of paper. Cut and paste carrots with singular nouns in the box labeled **Singular**. Cut and paste carrots with plural nouns in the box labeled **Plural**.

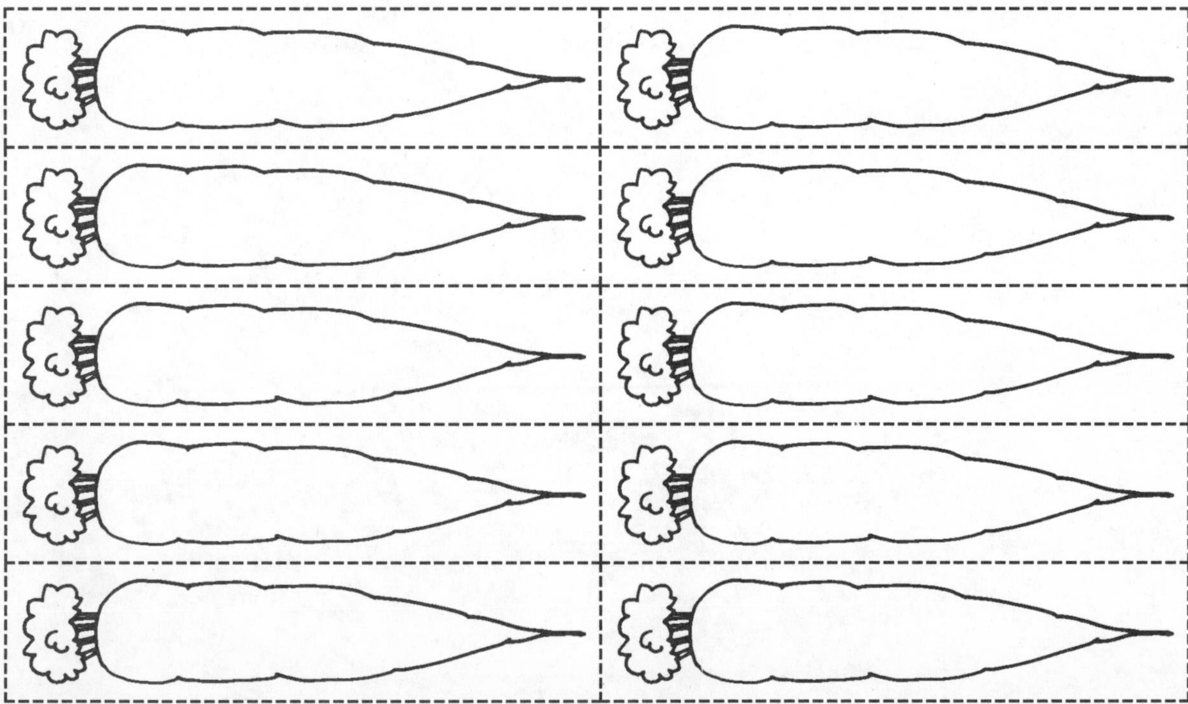

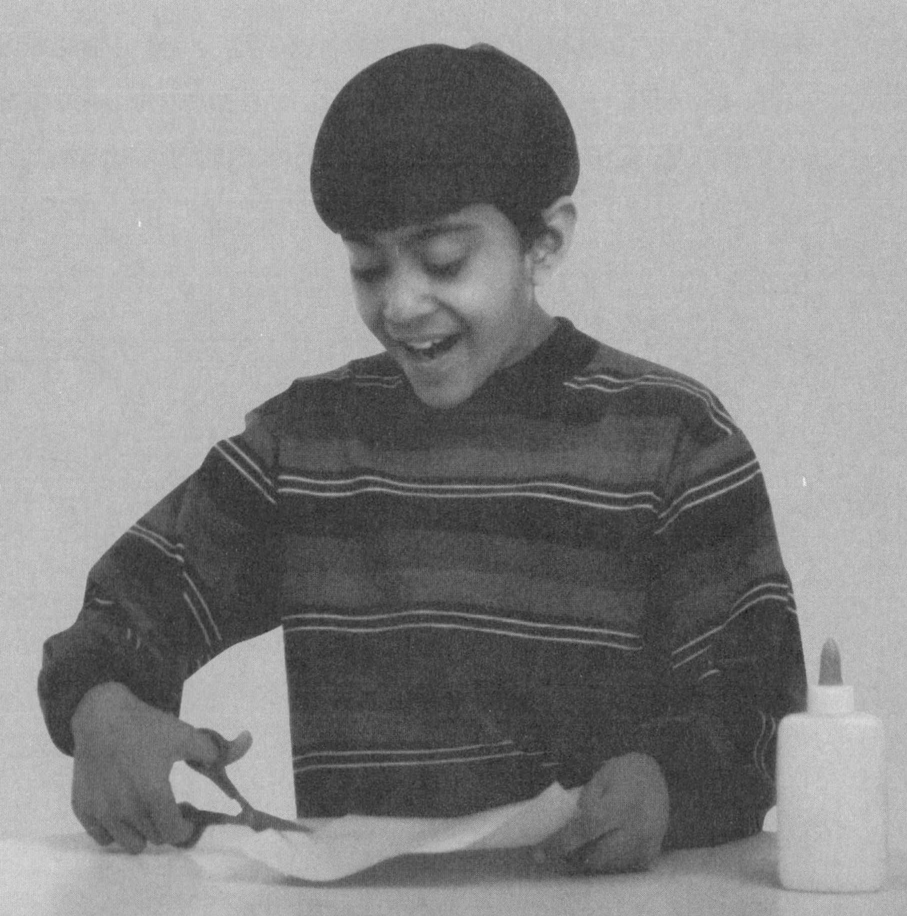

Name

A Letter to Ruby

Nouns

pear	pears	class	classes	penny	pennies	child	children
orange	oranges	bush	bushes	baby	babies	man	men
boy	boys	branch	branches	family	families	woman	women
		fox	foxes			mouse	mice
						tooth	teeth

Singular and Plural Nouns Help Sun Ho write a letter to Ruby. Write the plural form of each noun.

Dear Ruby,

I am very busy at the store. Every day I arrange the fruits and ________ (vegetable). I put the ________ (cherry) in little ________ (box). Whole ________ (family) come to buy ________ (orange) and ________ (peach). Sometimes the ________ (child) stay and watch me work.

I am doing some new things. We now sell ________ (glass) of fruit juice. We also have ________ (dish) of cooked vegetables.

All my ________ (wish) have come true! I hope that you and Trudy are well.

Sincerely,

Sun Ho

Sun Ho

Name

Save It, Trade It

Complete and cut out the trading card. Draw a picture of yourself on the back. Have fun trading with your classmates!

Name: ______________________________ Age: ______

Favorite things to do: ______________________________

____

____

When I write a book about my life, the first **scene** will be ______

____

____

Someone who has **inspired** me is______________________________

because______________________________

____

When I **recognize** someone I know, I______________________________

____

A very important **custom** in my family is______________________________

____

It is important because______________________________

____

Name

Family Fun

Carmen's family did many things together. Fill in the web with things they did.

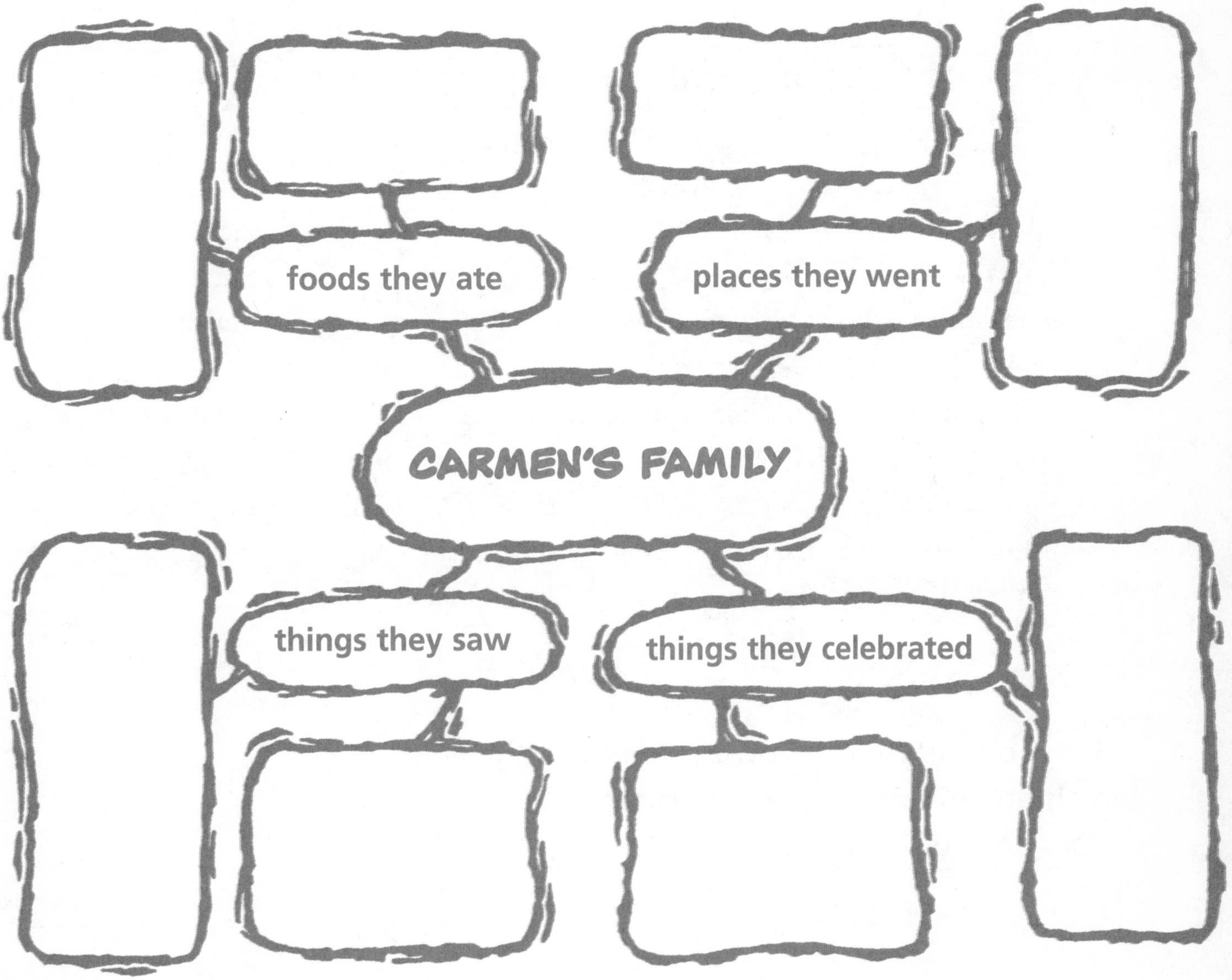

CARMEN'S FAMILY

foods they ate

places they went

things they saw

things they celebrated

Describe something that you do with your family.

Name

A Four-Star Review

Read the art review and answer the question.

Take a Look at These Pictures

by B. A. Critic
Staff

Carmen Lomas Garza's book, *Family Pictures/Cuadros de familia*, is filled with colorful paintings. She uses beautiful green and red paints to make her paintings bright. Her paintings are filled with realistic details so that people feel as though they are a part of the painting as they look at it.

The scenes that she paints show a family and the family's life in such a real way. Although this colorful book is called *Family Pictures/Cuadros de familia*, it's about so much more. Through her art, Carmen Lomas Garza takes us through the community where she was born and raised.

Based on this review, how do you think the author feels about Carmen Lomas Garza's artwork? How do you know this?

____

____

____

____

____

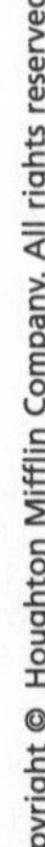

Name

A Journal of Your Own

Answer these questions. Then use the answers to start your own journal.

1. Write about something you heard or saw this week that made you laugh.

2. Look around you. Do you see anything that is pretty or unusual? Name the object and list a few words to describe it.

3. Name a song you like. Write a few words about how the song makes you feel.

4. Name one thing you would like to do or see someday.

Name

Compound Word Shuffle

Write the name of the picture on each card. Match a top card with a bottom card to find the word that fits each clue.

Example: In *Family Pictures/ Cuadros de familia*, Carmen saw this kind of shark at Padre Island.

hammer + 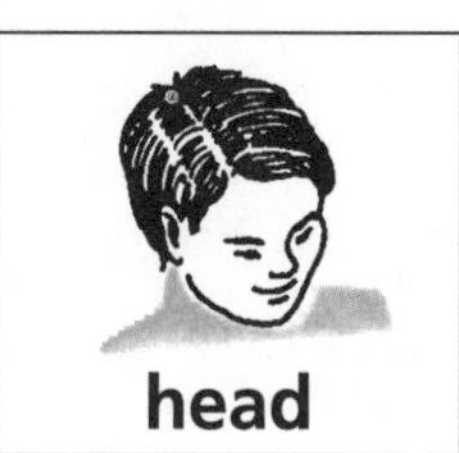
head = hammerhead

1. This kind of dough is used to make tamales. ______________________
2. A boy in the story passed one of these to his mother in church. ______________________
3. Carmen's grandfather brought this fruit one hot summer night. ______________________
4. The fisherman at Padre Island may have used one of these for bait. ______________________
5. This is a comfortable place to read a book. ______________________
6. You can ring this to be let inside. ______________________

Name ______________________________

Where Did It Go?

Choose the word that best fits with each pair. Then find and circle all twelve words in the word search.

scene	inspired
custom	recognize

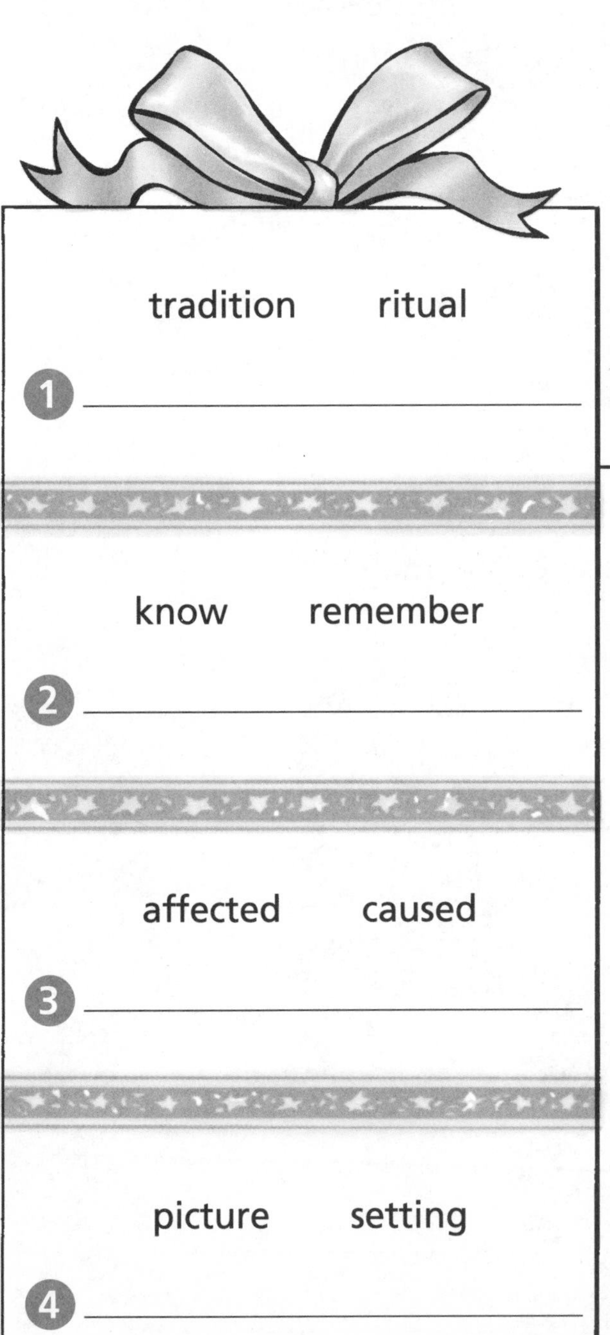

S	R	I	T	U	A	L	L	O	T	I
B	E	R	I	C	L	M	N	O	R	N
E	M	C	A	U	S	E	D	Z	A	S
R	E	C	O	G	N	I	Z	E	D	P
U	M	B	U	E	O	G	R	S	I	I
T	B	J	C	S	N	A	K	D	T	R
C	E	S	E	I	T	O	E	N	I	E
I	R	S	T	F	S	O	U	I	O	D
P	E	T	C	L	F	Z	M	Y	N	W
T	E	E	R	E	F	I	N	N	E	J
S	R	A	F	F	E	C	T	E	D	X

Name

Pick a Piñata

Spelling Words
1. **cook**
2. **knew**
3. **put**
4. **woods**
5. **pull**
6. **booth**
7. **coop**
8. **drew**

My Study List
What other words do you need to study for spelling? Add them to My Study List for *Family Pictures/ Cuadros de familia* in the back of this book.

Vowel Sounds in *cook* and *knew*

Some Spelling Words have the vowel sound that you hear in ***cook.*** This sound is written as /o͝o/. It may be spelled with the pattern ***oo*** or ***u.***

/o͝o/ cook put

The other Spelling Words have the vowel sound that you hear in ***knew.*** This sound is written as /o͞o/. It is often spelled with the pattern ***ew*** or ***oo.***

/o͞o/ knew booth

Write each Spelling Word in the piñata with the matching vowel sound.

Name

Spelling Spree

Proofreading Find and circle four misspelled Spelling Words in this family's list of things to do before an outdoor party. Then write each word correctly.

Spelling Words

1. cook
2. knew
3. put
4. woods
5. pull
6. booth
7. coop
8. drew

1. Gather the chickens and put them in their coup.
2. Cut the grass and pul weeds out of the flower beds.
3. Set up the boothe for the artist who drue funny pictures last year.

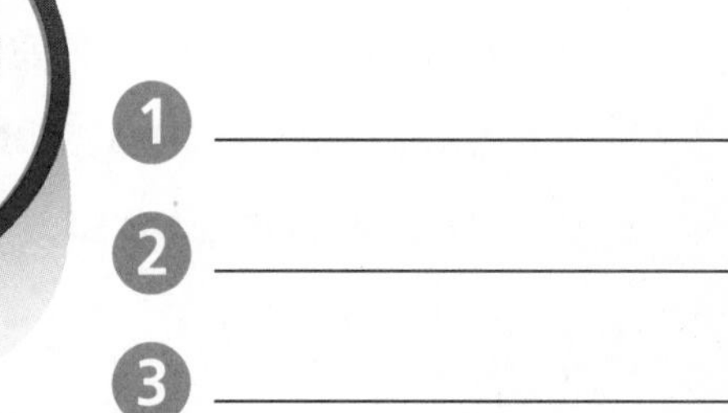

1 ____________
2 ____________
3 ____________
4 ____________

A Family Trip Write a Spelling Word to take the place of the underlined word or words in each sentence.

5 I thought you already <u>had the facts</u> about the plans for our family camping trip. ____________

6 We will <u>heat</u> all our meals over a campfire. ____________

7 We can look for snakes and frogs in the <u>forest</u> near the lake. ____________

8 Meet us early so we can find a great spot to <u>place</u> our tents! ____________

From a Fan Which of Carmen Lomas Garza's pictures did you like best? Write a short letter telling her what you liked about it. Use Spelling Words from the list.

Name ______________________________

Win the Prize!

Singular Possessives	Plural Possessives
mother's voice	mothers' voices
fox's ears	foxes' ears
lady's ring	ladies' rings

Possessive Nouns Many families enjoy fairs. Play the Possessive Nouns game at this fair. First, decide if the nouns in parentheses are singular or plural. Then write their possessive forms.

1. The __________________ booths and events are fun. (fair) *1 point*

2. __________________ tacos taste good. (Carlos) *2 points*

3. The __________________ favorite game was the fishing game. (girl) *3 points*

4. They try to hook the paper __________________ heads. (fishes) *4 points*

5. We visited the __________________ cages. (bunnies) *5 points*

6. One naughty child tried to pull the __________________ tail. (pony) *6 points*

7. We liked one __________________ big brown eyes. (calf) *7 points*

8. The __________________ parents were looking for them. (boys) *8 points*

Add Them Up! You need 15 points in three tries to win a teddy bear! Which three boards would you have to hit to make 15 points? Write the numbers in the bears.

Name

Family Photo Album

Possessive Nouns Write a sentence to tell about each picture in this family album. Make the noun beside each picture possessive, and use it in your sentence.

1 puppies

2 baby

3 Nat

4 Felix

5 Elissa

6 Grandmother

1 ______________________

2 ______________________

3 ______________________

4 ______________________

5 ______________________

6 ______________________

Name

Curious Questions

Fill in the survey by checking the two words that have nearly the same meaning. Then answer the questions.

1 ☐ title fight ☐ championship ☐ practice

2 Describe how you might feel if you won a **title fight**.

____

____

3 ☐ yelled ☐ whispered ☐ bellowed

4 When have you **bellowed** when you should not have?

____

5 ☐ eased ☐ braced ☐ relaxed

6 Describe a time when you **braced** yourself.

____

____

7 ☐ unknown ☐ name ☐ title

8 Do you have a favorite **title?** What is it?

____

9 ☐ tattered ☐ new ☐ unused

10 Would the President wear **tattered** clothes? Why or why not?

____

____

11 ☐ whirl ☐ stop ☐ spin

12 How would you feel after you **whirled** around a room?

____

Name

What's It About?

Complete the summary for the book jacket for *When Jo Louis Won the Title.*

When Jo Louis Won the Title

Jo Louis is worried about going to a new school because ______________________________

____

To help her, John Henry ______________________________

____

When John Henry first got to Harlem, ______________________________

____

People were celebrating because ______________________________

____

That night was special to John Henry because ______________________________

____

Jo Louis is still a little scared when she goes to school. But on that first day, ______________________________

____

Name ________________

Get in the Ring

Look at the pictures and answer the questions.

1 What general statement can you make about a boxer's typical day?

____

____

____

____

____

2 What general statement can you make about boxing rings?

____

____

____

____

____

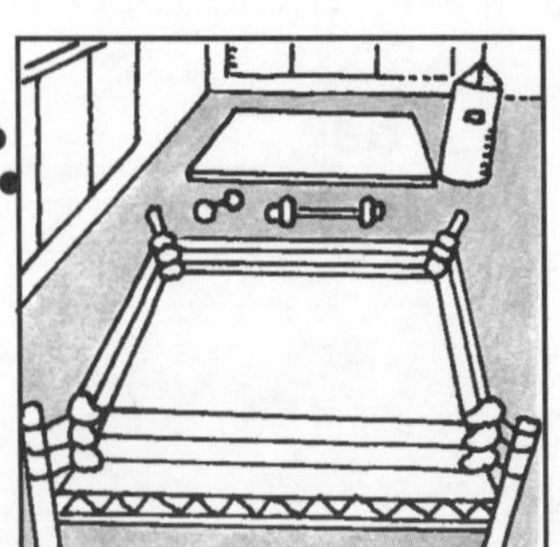

Name

What's the Story?

Read the story about how this puppy got her name. Find the five pairs of sentences that have the same predicates. Combine the sentences in each pair by making a compound subject with the word *and*. Write the new sentences on the lines below.

My dog is named "Shoe." Her name has a story. My brother really wanted a puppy. I really wanted a puppy. My parents said, "No way!" My brother begged them. I begged them. We finally convinced them.

We brought the puppy home. My family ate dinner. The puppy ate dinner. She ate from a little bowl under the table. Suddenly, we heard growling. My brother looked down. I looked down. The puppy was chewing a hole in Dad's shoe! Dad looked mad. Mom looked mad. In one week, our new puppy ruined seven perfectly good shoes!

Dad started calling her "Shoe." It may seem like a weird name for a dog, but like a shoe, it just seemed to fit!

1 ______________________________

2 ______________________________

3 ______________________________

4 ______________________________

5 ______________________________

Name

Contraction Puzzle

Jo Louis learned something important from her grandfather. Solve the puzzle to find out what she learned. Write the two words that each contraction is made from. Then write each numbered letter on the line with the matching number below.

1. we're ___ ___ ___ ___ ___ (13, 4)
2. doesn't ___ ___ ___ ___ ___ ___ ___ (9)
3. you're ___ ___ ___ ___ ___ ___ (5, 17)
4. I've ___ ___ ___ ___ ___ (11, 2)
5. mustn't ___ ___ ___ ___ ___ ___ ___ (8, 14)
6. she's ___ ___ ___ ___ ___ (1, 12)
7. needn't ___ ___ ___ ___ ___ ___ ___ (6, 16)
8. they've ___ ___ ___ ___ ___ ___ ___ ___ (3, 10, 7)
9. couldn't ___ ___ ___ ___ ___ ___ ___ ___ (15)
10. you'll ___ ___ ___ ___ ___ ___ ___ (18)

What Jo Louis learned from her grandfather:

___ ___ ___ ___ ___ ___ ___ ___ ___
1 2 3 4 5 6 7 8 9

___ ___ ___ ___ ___ ___ ___ ___ ___.
10 11 12 13 14 15 16 17 18

Name

All Crossed Up

Complete the puzzle with words from the box.

whirled	title fight	title	tattered	bellowed
braced	jazz	Harlem	daydream	perched

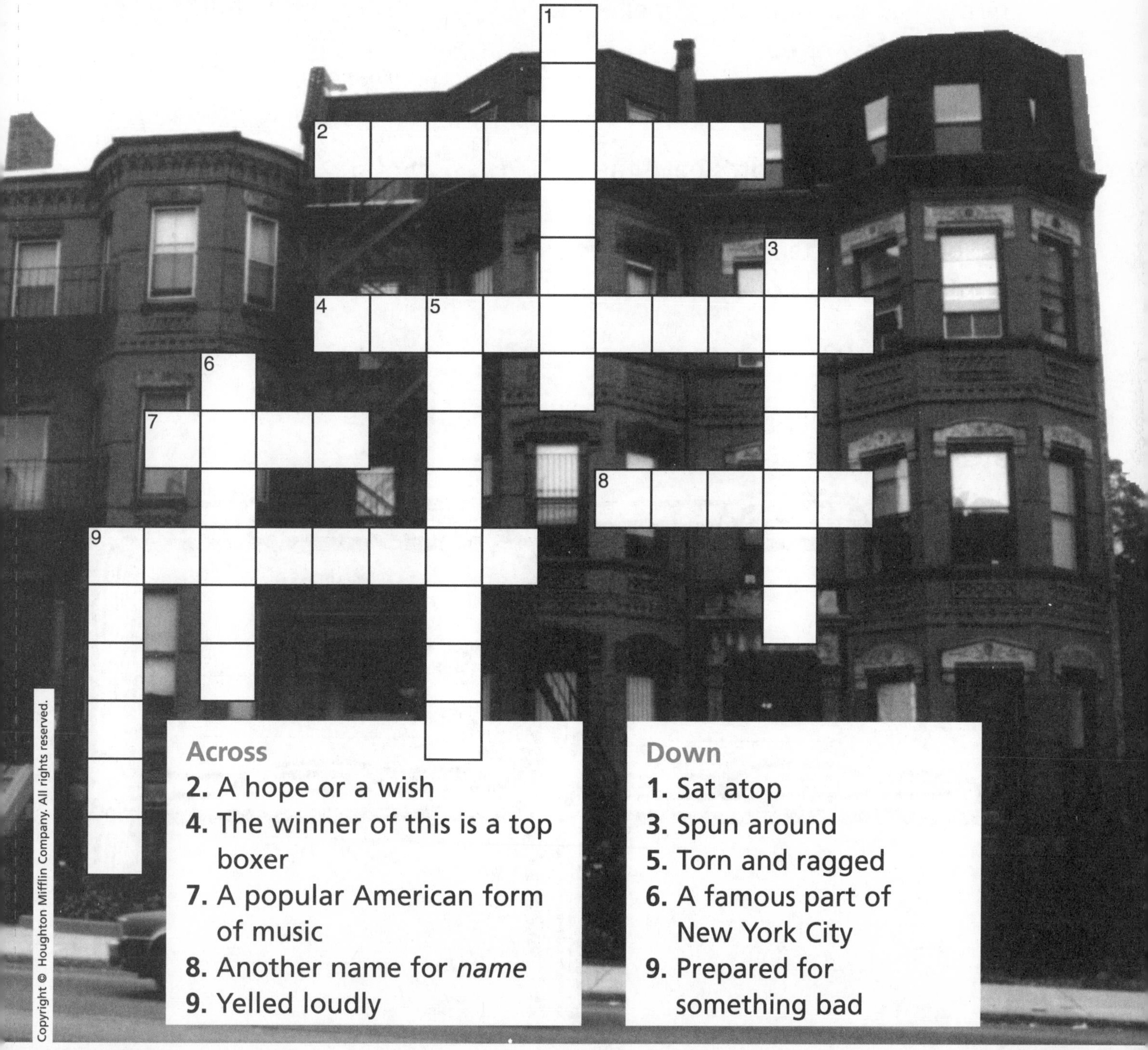

1 2 3 4 5 6 7 8 9

Across

2. A hope or a wish

4. The winner of this is a top boxer

7. A popular American form of music

8. Another name for *name*

9. Yelled loudly

Down

1. Sat atop

3. Spun around

5. Torn and ragged

6. A famous part of New York City

9. Prepared for something bad

Name

Moving Day

Vowel Sounds in *town* and *boy*

Some Spelling Words have the vowel sound that you hear in ***town.*** This sound is written as /ou/. It is often spelled with the pattern ***ow*** or ***ou.***

/ou/ town proud

The other Spelling Words have the vowel sound that you hear in ***boy.*** This sound is written as /oi/. It is spelled with the pattern ***oi*** or ***oy.***

/oi/ noise boy

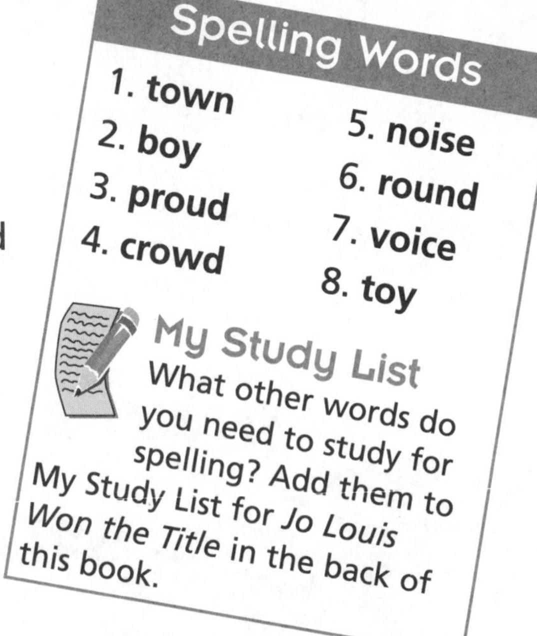

Write each Spelling Word on the suitcase that has the matching sound and spelling pattern.

Name

Spelling Spree

Spelling Words	
1. town	5. noise
2. boy	6. round
3. proud	7. voice
4. crowd	8. toy

A Proud Title Write a Spelling Word to fit each clue.

1. a large group of people ___ ___ ___ [___] ___
2. what you use to speak ___ ___ [___] ___ ___
3. a place smaller than a city ___ ___ ___ [___]
4. the shape of a circle ___ ___ ___ [___] ___
5. a sound ___ ___ ___ ___ [___]
6. pleased with oneself ___ [___] ___ ___ ___

What word describes the boxer Joe Louis? To find out, write the boxed letters in order.

___ ___ ___ ___ ___ ___

Proofreading Find and circle four misspelled Spelling Words in this post card. Then write each word correctly.

Dear Etta,
When are you coming to town? I want to show you my new school. Today I met a nice bouy who liked my name and my singing vois. You'd be prowd of me—I shared my new toi with him!
Love, J. L.

7. ________________
8. ________________
9. ________________
10. ________________

Name Me If you could choose a new name for yourself, what would it be? On a separate piece of paper, explain your choice. Use Spelling Words from the list.

Name

Window Words

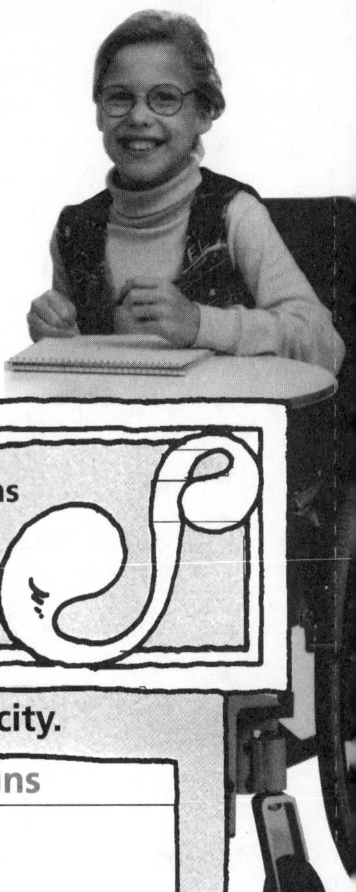

Common and Proper Nouns Find the nouns in each sentence. Write the proper nouns in the windows on the left. Write the common nouns in the windows on the right. Remember to use capital letters with proper nouns.

Nouns

proper nouns	common nouns
Jo Louis	girl
Chicago	city
Friday	day

The writer, ms. rochelle, wrote about new york city.

proper nouns	common nouns

The neighborhood called harlem was named for a town in holland.

proper nouns	common nouns

Many cars cross the bridges over the hudson river.

proper nouns	common nouns

Name

Trying Tongue Twisters Together

Common and Proper Nouns Jo and John Henry are trying tongue twisters. Write each tongue twister correctly. Begin each proper noun with a capital letter.

1. carl and carol live on the corner of court street.

2. polly patter plays with a polliwog in potter pond.

3. mr. marker marks meat at mark's market.

4. fido's favorite food is called fudgy fig fingers.

Now write a tongue twister of your own. Use capital letters with nouns correctly.

5.

Name

A Special Day

Do any of these ideas spark memories of your own?

A fun trip

An accident

Playing on a team

Moving to a new place

Ideas for My Story About Myself

Write three to five ideas for a story about yourself.

____

____

____

____

____

Think about each idea on your list. Ask yourself these questions.

Can I remember this experience clearly?

Why do I want to write about it?

Circle the story idea you want to write about.

Name

Do You Remember?

Close your eyes and picture your story.
Write notes that answer these questions.

Who else is in your story?

Where does it take place?

What happens?

Draw the most important part of your story in this circle. Make your picture as detailed as possible.

Name

Making It Better

Revising Checklist

Ask yourself these questions about your story.

- ❑ Does my story have a beginning, a middle, and an end?
- ❑ Does the beginning lead quickly into the main event?
- ❑ Do all my sentences keep to the topic?
- ❑ Did I use details so that my readers can picture what happened?

Questions for a Writing Conference

Use these questions to help you discuss your story with a classmate.

- What is best about this story?
- Does the story begin in an interesting way?
- Which parts do not keep to the topic?
- Which parts are hard to picture? What details are needed?
- How did the people feel? Are more details needed?

Write notes to help you remember the ideas from your writing conference.

My Notes

____

____

____

____

____

____

____

____

Name

A Great Place to Live

Write a magazine ad about the community you liked most in Community Ties. Fill out the chart to help you plan your ad.

List three things that you liked most about the people, places, and activities of the community you picked.

1 ______________________________

2 ______________________________

3 ______________________________

Show what is special about the community. Follow these directions:

1. Fold a sheet of drawing paper in half to make two magazine pages.

2. On one page, draw pictures of the three things you wrote about in the chart.

3. On the other page, write a slogan. Make your slogan a generalization. Include words such as *all*, *always*, *everyone*, *many*, or *most*.

4. On the same page as your slogan, write details about your pictures.

Checklist **Use this list to check your work.**

- ❑ My ad shows people, places, and activities.
- ❑ My slogan is a generalization.
- ❑ My ad gives details about the community.

Name

Disaster!

Cut out a picture of a disaster from a magazine or a newspaper and paste it on this page. Then answer the questions.

1 What makes this event a disaster?

2 Why did the disaster occur?

3 Could anything have been done to prevent the disaster? If so, what?

Name

Disaster!

As you read each selection in Disaster!, fill in the boxes of the chart that apply to the selection.

	What was unexpected about the disaster?	What did people learn from the disaster?
The *Titanic:* Lost . . . and Found		
Pompeii . . . Buried Alive!		
Patrick and the Great Molasses Explosion		

Name

Everybody Remain Calm

Read the ship's emergency instructions and answer the questions.

To all passengers:

If there are any problems during this **voyage**, follow these instructions:

☆ Obey the captain's **orders** at all times.

☆ Head for the nearest lifeboat.

☆ When you are in a lifeboat, wait for the **rescue** ship to come to you.

☆ Don't panic. If you follow all of the instructions, we will all be **survivors**.

1. Why would these instructions be for the **passengers**? ______

2. Why might someone go on a **voyage**? ______

3. Why should people follow the captain's **orders** at all times? ______

4. How would a **rescue** ship do its job? ______

5. Why would the people who don't panic be **survivors**? ______

Name

Titanic Found!

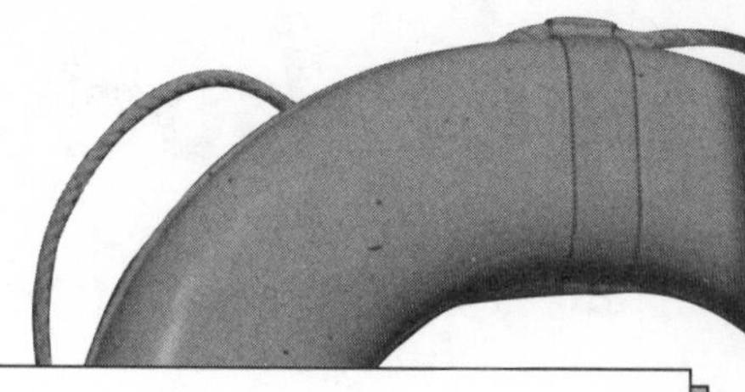

Rewrite the article so that the details are correct.

Ballard Finds *Titanic*

Wire Report

Robert Ballard found the *Titanic* today. The *Titanic* had been lying on the bottom of the Pacific Ocean since April 15, 1972. On that day, while on its second voyage, the *Titanic* hit another ship and sank.

Luckily, the *Titanic* had enough lifeboats for all its passengers, so everybody on the ship survived. The survivors were brought to safety by helicopter.

Ballard's discovery is very exciting. Now Ballard says that he wants to bring the *Titanic* to the surface so that he can recover the *Titanic*'s treasure.

Name

Treasure Hunt

Read the page from the instruction book. Write the topic of the page, the main idea of paragraph one, and three details that support the main idea.

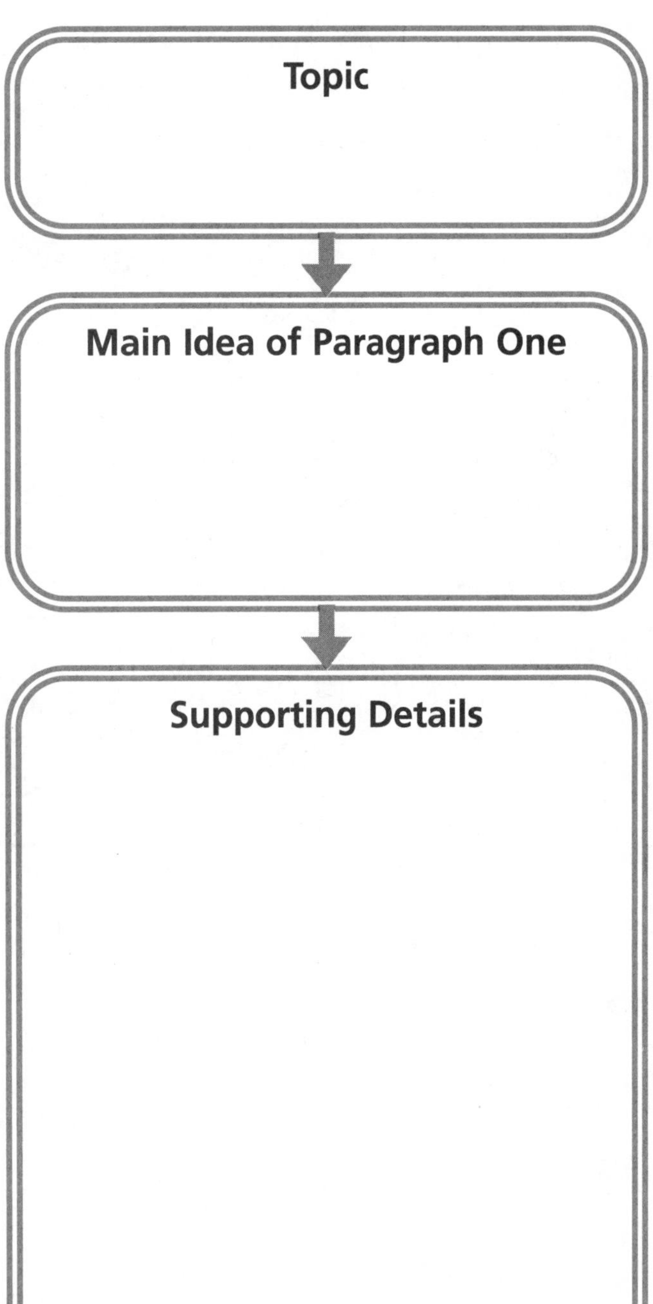

How to Find Sunken Treasure

Patience is a very important part of hunting for sunken treasure. Often, you can search for many years and not find the treasure you want. You can sometimes find a small part of your treasure but still be far away from the main part. Sometimes, you can even see things that look like your treasure but really aren't.

When you have finally found your treasure, be very careful. Do not touch the treasure until you have taken pictures of it in the water. Keep a careful record of each piece of the treasure. The ship itself must be treated carefully because it can crumble if it is exposed to the air.

On a separate sheet of paper, copy and complete the graphic organizer for paragraph two.

Name

Iceberg Ahead!

Find the sentences in the icebergs that have the same subjects. Write them as one sentence with a compound predicate.

Glaciers break apart.

The Coast Guard keeps an eye on icebergs.

An iceberg's ice is very hard.

Icebergs come from glaciers.

Glaciers push toward the sea.

An iceberg's ice can be over a thousand years old.

The Coast Guard warns ships about them.

Icebergs are made of fresh water.

1 ______________________________

____

2 ______________________________

____

3 ______________________________

____

4 ______________________________

____

Name

Silver Lining

The sinking of the *Titanic* was a disaster, but it had one good result. Find out what that result was by solving the puzzle. For each definition, write a word made from a base word in the box and the ending *-er* or *-est.* Then write each numbered letter on the line with the matching number.

teach	strong	hard	fast	heavy
smart	hike	sleepy	pitch	travel

1. weighing more ___ ___ ___(2) ___ ___ ___ ___
2. one who goes on a trip ___ ___ ___ ___ ___ ___ ___ ___(5)
3. moving most quickly ___(3) ___ ___ ___ ___ ___ ___
4. more tired ___ ___ ___ ___ ___(9) ___ ___ ___
5. one who climbs a mountain ___(7) ___ ___ ___ ___
6. one who helps others learn ___ ___(4) ___ ___ ___ ___ ___
7. more wise ___(6) ___ ___ ___ ___ ___ ___
8. one who throws to a batter ___ ___(8) ___ ___ ___ ___ ___
9. most difficult ___ ___ ___ ___ ___ ___(10) ___
10. most powerful ___(1) ___ ___ ___ ___ ___ ___ ___ ___

What the world gained from the *Titanic* disaster:

___(1) ___(2) ___(3) ___(4) ___(5)   ___(6) ___(7) ___(8) ___(9) ___(10)

Name ______________________

Loading the Ship

captain	crow's-nest
decks	lifeboats
passengers	rescue ship
submarine	survivors
voyage	

Fill in the levels of the ship with the correct words. Some words can fit in more than one level. Then add some of your own words to each level.

Things That Go in Water

1. ______________________ 4. ______________________
2. ______________________ 5. ______________________
3. ______________________

Words That Mean "Trip"

1. ______________________ 2. ______________________

Parts of a Ship

1. ______________________ 3. ______________________
2. ______________________ 4. ______________________

People on a Ship

1. ______________________ 3. ______________________
2. ______________________ 4. ______________________

People Who Give Orders

1. ______________________ 3. ______________________
2. ______________________

Name

Safe and Sound

The Vowel Sound in *saw* Each Spelling Word has the vowel sound that you hear in ***saw.*** This sound is written as |ô|. It can be spelled with the pattern ***aw, a* before *l*, *ough,*** or ***augh.***

|ô| saw talk thought caught

Help save the passengers! Write the Spelling Words that match the pattern for the |ô| sound shown on each lifeboat.

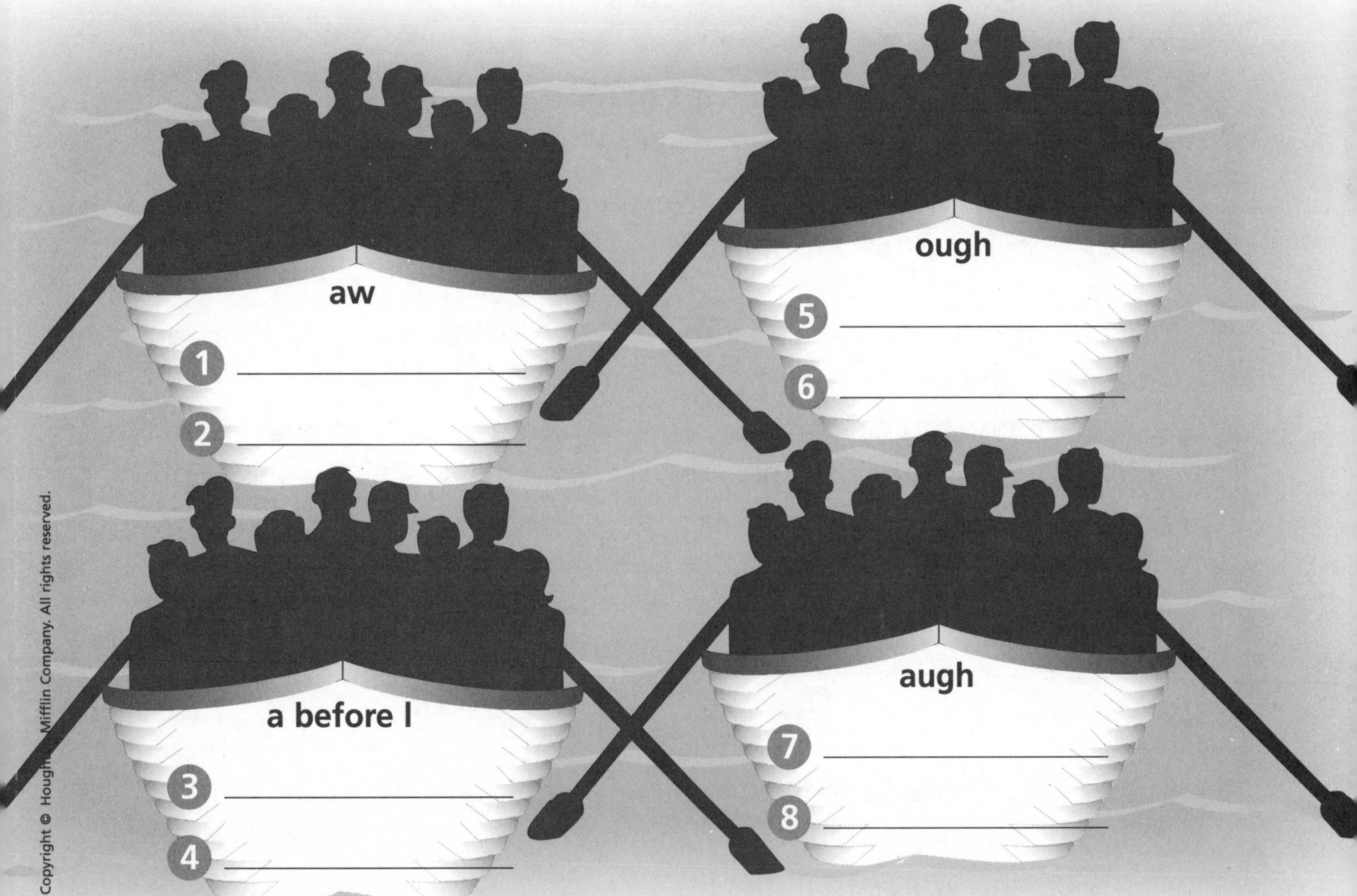

Spelling Words

1. saw
2. talk
3. small
4. thought
5. law
6. caught
7. fought
8. taught

My Study List
What other words do you need to study for spelling? Add them to My Study List for *The Titanic: Lost . . . and Found* in the back of this book.

aw

1 ______

2 ______

ough

5 ______

6 ______

a before l

3 ______

4 ______

augh

7 ______

8 ______

Name

Spelling Spree

Spelling Words

1. saw
2. talk
3. small
4. thought
5. law
6. caught
7. fought
8. taught

Proofreading Find and circle four misspelled Spelling Words in these headlines. Then write each word correctly. Begin each word with a capital letter.

Ship's Radio Cawt Sinking Boat's Signal for Help

1 ______________

Rescuers Saw Smal Boats in Time to Save Hundreds of People!

2 ______________

Sailors Faught to Have More Lifeboat Drills

3 ______________

New Lawe Passed to Make Ships Safer

4 ______________

Safety Senses Write a Spelling Word to complete each sentence in this part of a news story.

After the ship sank, a teenage girl (5) a little boy fall out of a lifeboat. The girl had been (6) what to do in swim class, so she held an oar out to the (7) boy. He (8) hold of it and was pulled to safety. The teenager would not (9) to reporters. However, the boy said that he (10) the girl should get a medal.

5 ______________ 7 ______________ 9 ______________

6 ______________ 8 ______________ 10 ______________

SOS Your ship sank and you're on an island. On a separate sheet of paper, tell what happened and where you are. Use Spelling Words from the list.

Name

Voyage of the Verbs

Singular Noun in the Subject
A flag waves.

Plural Noun in the Subject
Many flags wave.

Verbs in the Present Read each sentence. Write the correct present-time form of the verb in ( ).

1. The *Titanic* _______________ on the ocean bottom. (sit)
2. Scientists _______________ a different route. (try)
3. Robert Ballard _______________ a special underwater robot. (invent)
4. The *Argo* _______________ very, very deep. (dive)
5. The *Argo* _______________ the sea bottom. (reach)
6. The robot _______________ away the sand. (push)
7. A fish _______________ by the ship. (pass)
8. The explorers _______________ the *Titanic*! (find)
9. Giant anchors _______________ in the sand. (rest)
10. The message _______________ that the ship be left in peace. (ask)

Name

Disasters in the Present

Verbs in the Present Picture in your mind a disaster at sea. First, draw your scene on the canvas.

Next, write at least five complete sentences about your picture. Use a verb in present time in each sentence. Use three verbs from the suggestion box.

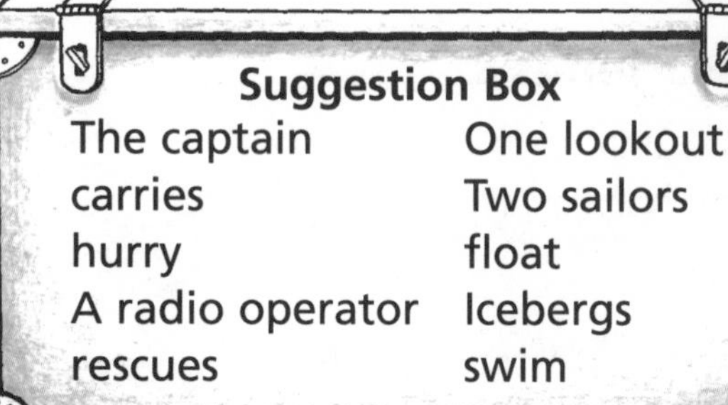

Name

Outburst!

Words are erupting from this volcano! Cut out and paste the words next to their meanings.

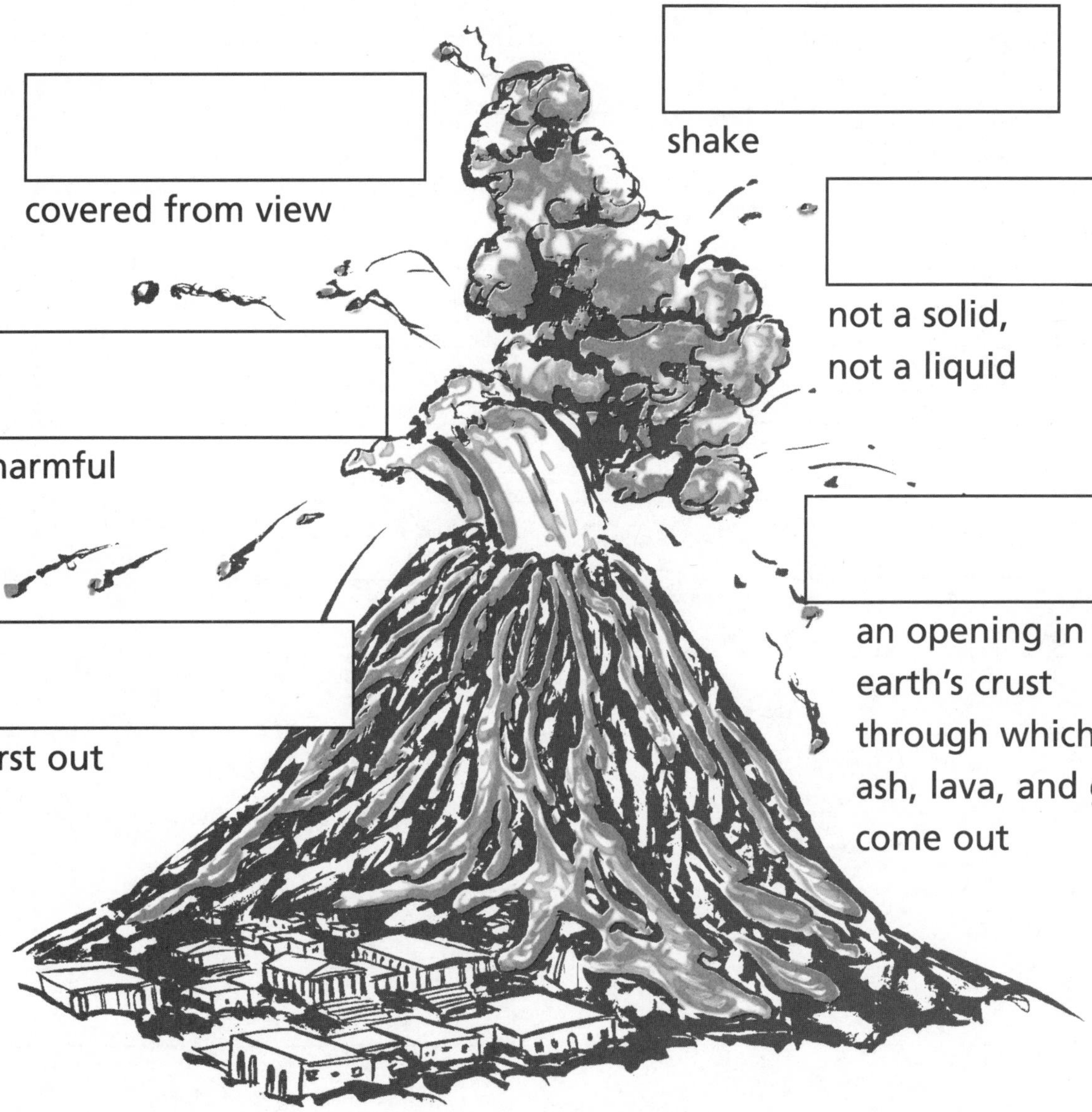

covered from view

shake

not a solid, not a liquid

harmful

an opening in the earth's crust through which ash, lava, and gas come out

burst out

Use these words to write about a volcano on the back of this sheet.

volcano	gas	erupted
tremble	poisonous	buried

Write about a volcano.

Name

Trapped in Time

Finish the index cards.

Three things people in Pompeii did every day were

____

____

____

____

____

____

Three things that happened when Vesuvius erupted were

____

____

____

____

____

____

We know about Pompeii because

____

____

____

____

____

____

Two things that scientists found were

____

____

____

____

____

Name

Post Card from Pompeii

Read the post card. Find four facts and four opinions. Write them in the chart. Then answer the question.

Dear Jeff,

Pompeii is a very interesting place to visit. It was once covered with volcanic ash. But scientists have done a good job of uncovering it. They have found jewelry and unbroken eggs here. They even found a mosaic that says "Beware of Dog" in Latin. These aren't even the most amazing parts of Pompeii. The city has been partially rebuilt. You should try to visit Pompeii.

See you soon!

María

FACTS	OPINIONS

What are two ways you can prove these facts?

Name

Can You Explain It?

Use this page to plan your explanation. Then number the facts in the order you will use them.

Topic:

Topic Sentence:

Fact:

Fact:

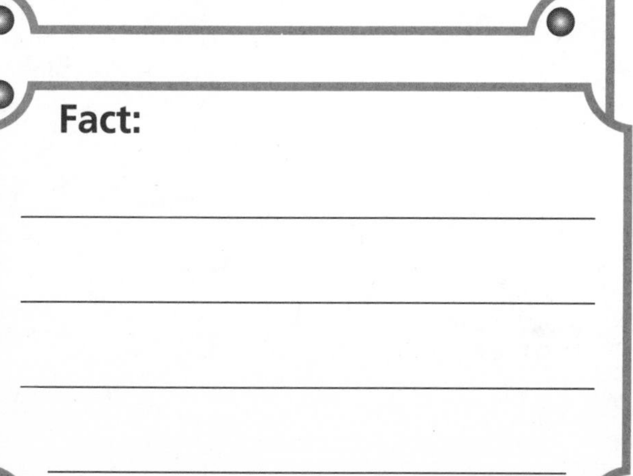

Fact:

Fact:

Name ______________________________

Dig It!

To find out what the scientists uncovered at Pompeii, solve the puzzle. First, divide each word into two syllables. Write the syllables on the lines with the dot between them.

	Word	First syllable		Second syllable
1	captures	____________	•	____________ 5
2	mainland	____________ 6	•	____________
3	subjects	____________	•	____________ 3
4	mammals	____________	•	____________ 9
5	picnic	____________ 4	•	____________
6	purple	____________	•	____________ 7
7	annoy	____________ 1	•	____________
8	explode	____________	•	____________
9	oblong	____________ 2	•	____________
10	anger	____________ 8	•	____________

Write each numbered syllable on the line with the matching number.

What the scientists found:

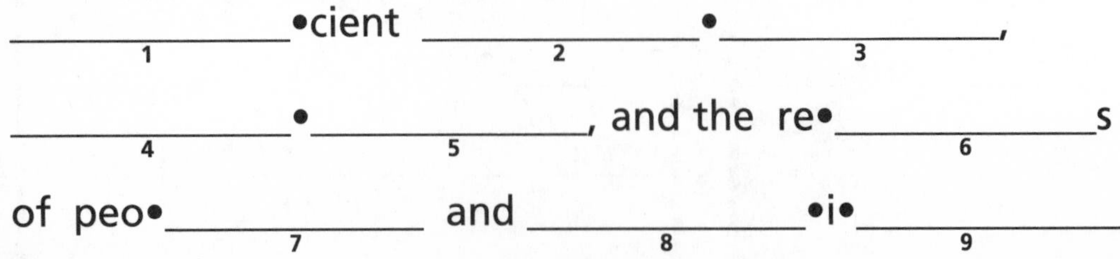

____________ (1) •cient ____________ (2) •____________ (3),

____________ (4) •____________ (5), and the re•____________ (6) s

of peo•____________ (7) and ____________ (8) •i•____________ (9)

Name

Pompeii Puzzle

Complete the puzzle by using the clues.

ashes	buried	enormous	erupted	pebbles	poisonous
sealed	skeletons	spilled	trapped	tremble	volcano

Across

2. Groups of bones
5. What Vesuvius did
7. Some people of Pompeii were ____ under rocks and ashes from Vesuvius.
9. Shake violently
10. Dusty material that came out of Vesuvius
11. A cloud of ____ gas came out of Vesuvius.

Down

1. Shut tightly
2. Poured out
3. Caught
4. Little, tiny rocks
6. Very large
8. An explosive mountain

Name

Dark Days

Spelling Words

1. dark
2. more
3. start
4. story
5. near
6. morning
7. part
8. year

My Study List
What other words do you need to study for spelling? Add them to My Study List for *Pompeii . . . Buried Alive!* in the back of this book.

Vowel + *r* Sounds Each Spelling Word has a vowel sound + ***r***. The vowel + ***r*** sounds you hear in ***dark*** are written as |är|. They can be spelled with the pattern ***ar***.

|är| dark

The vowel + ***r*** sounds you hear in ***near*** are written as |îr|. They can be spelled with the pattern ***ear***.

|îr| near

The vowel + ***r*** sounds you hear in ***more*** are written as |ôr|. They can be spelled with the patterns ***or*** and ***ore***.

|ôr| story more

Write each Spelling Word on the cloud with the matching vowel sound.

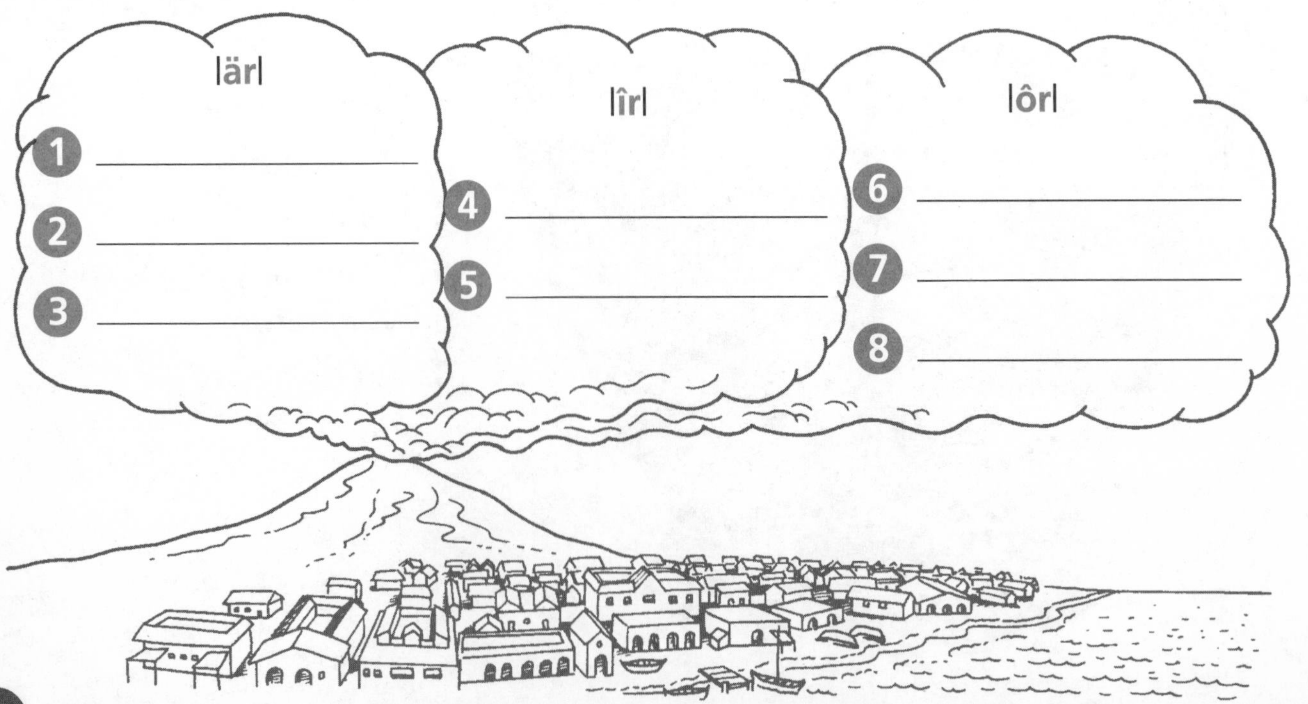

Name

Spelling Spree

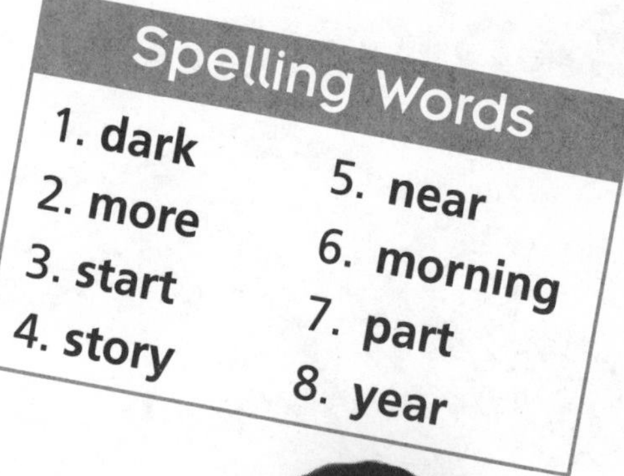

Only Opposites The second part of each clue is the opposite of the first part. Write the Spelling Word that fits each clue.

1. not far, but ____________
2. not light, but ____________
3. not whole, but ____________
4. not stop, but ____________
5. not evening, but ____________
6. not less, but ____________

Proofreading Find and circle four misspelled Spelling Words on this sign at a museum. Then write each word correctly.

One morening near the town of Pompeii, Mount Vesuvius blew its top. Ashes piled up higher than the second storey of some houses. Thick, darck clouds filled the sky. In two days the whole town was buried. More than a yeer later the volcano still erupted, but Pompeii was gone.

7. ____________
8. ____________
9. ____________
10. ____________

Danger Signs On a separate sheet of paper, draw three signs to warn people of danger. Below each sign, write one or two sentences that tell what the sign means. Use Spelling Words from the list.

Name ....

Explosion!

Present	Spelling Change	Past Time
melt	+ ed	melt**ed**
explode	– e + ed	explod**ed**
drop	+ p + ed	drop**ped**
hurry	– y + i + ed	hurr**ied**

Read the sentences. Write the correct past time form of the verb in ( ) to complete each sentence.

1. The falling rock ________________ everything in its path. (crush)
2. The family ________________ their best silver and dishes. (carry)
3. Some people ________________ nothing from the burning ashes. (save)
4. Others ________________ for help from the gods. (cry)
5. The shower of hot ashes ________________ a long time. (last)
6. The rumbling finally ________________. (stop)
7. Someone ________________ to save a lost dog. (try)
8. We ________________ a terrible lesson about the volcanoes. (learn)
9. Across the bay, a boy ________________ at the strange sight. (gaze)
10. His letters ________________ the disaster of Pompeii. (describe)

Name

Uncovering the Past

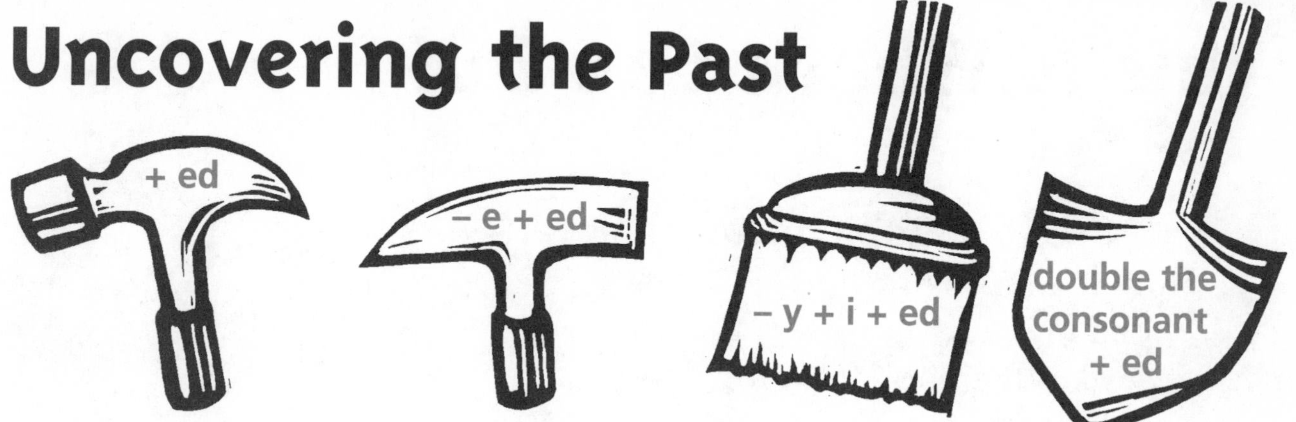

Help scientists uncover the ruins of Pompeii. Choose the right tool for forming the past time verb. Every time you write a correct verb, you get closer to Pompeii. The first stone has been uncovered for you.

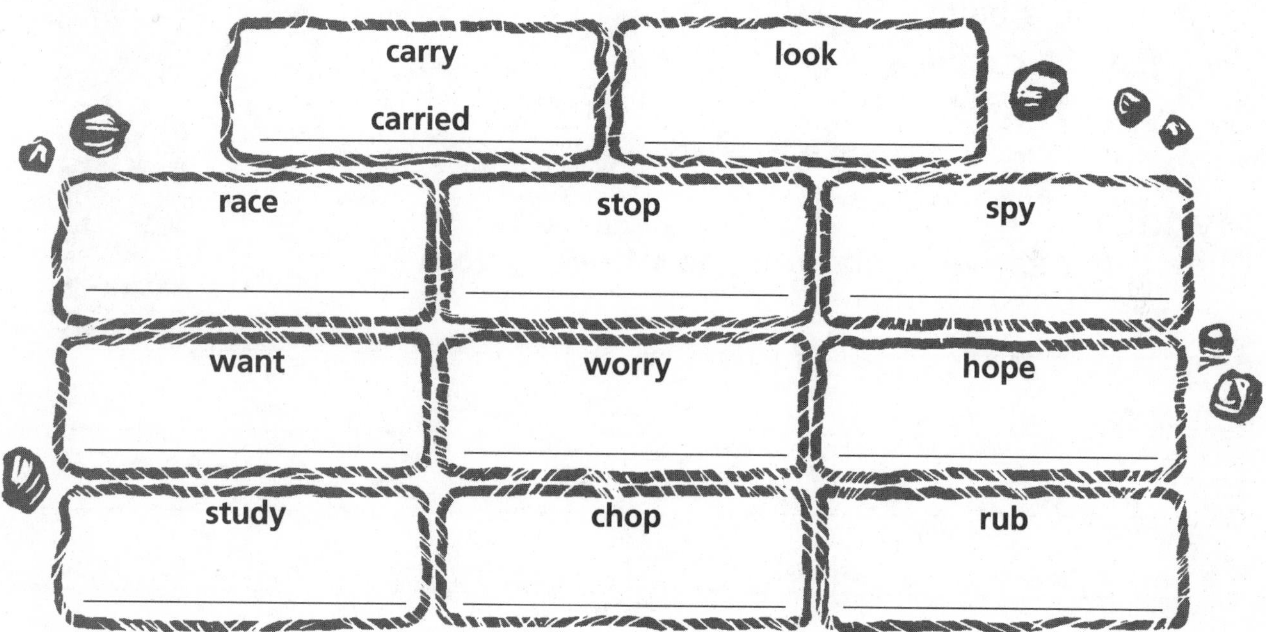

Write sentences for five of the verbs you wrote.

1 ______

2 ______

3 ______

4 ______

5 ______

Name

This Is What I Can Do!

Topic Ideas

How to . . .

feed my cat
check out a book from the library
use the computer's Cut and Paste features
make a paper airplane
grow crystals
make a piñata
weave a belt
make a rubber stamp
play dodge ball

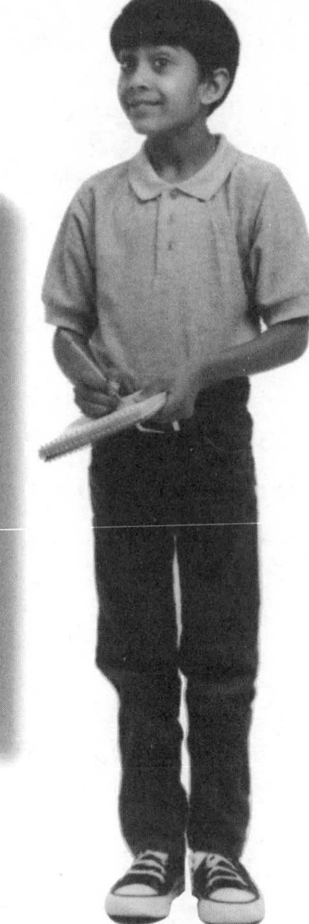

My Ideas

Write three to five things you know how to do well.

1 ______________________

2 ______________________

3 ______________________

4 ______________________

5 ______________________

Think about each idea. Ask yourself these questions.

Can I explain all of the steps clearly?

Do I really want to write about this topic?

Do I know exactly how to do this?

Circle the idea you want to write about.

Name

Step by Step

Write your topic. Then make notes in words or pictures to answer each question.

My topic is

What materials are needed?

What are the steps?

Step 1

Step 2

Step 3

Step 4

Step 5

Name

Take Another Look

Reread and revise your instructions.

Revising Checklist

Use these questions to help you revise your paper.

- ☐ Did I begin my instructions with a topic sentence?
- ☐ Did I include all steps?
- ☐ Did I give complete details?
- ☐ Is the order of the steps correct?
- ☐ Did I use order words?

Questions for a Writing Conference

Use these questions to discuss your paper with a classmate.

- What do you like about these instructions?
- Is it clear what the instructions are for?
- Are sizes, amounts, and colors of the materials given?
- Are the steps complete and in order?
- What other information is needed?

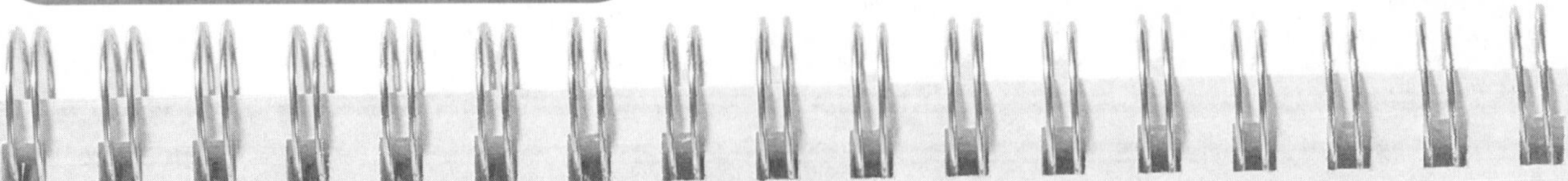

Notes from My Writing Conference with

____
Classmate's Name

____

____

____

____

____

____

____

Name

Sticky Scene

Use the words to describe what you see in the picture.

gooey **molasses** **barrels** **craving** **pitcher**

Name

Map Madness

Write which characters were at each place and what they were doing when the molasses tank exploded.

The Loading Docks

Outside the Molasses Store

Patrick's House

Name

A Sweet Story

Cut and paste the correct picture in the box. Then complete each statement of cause and effect.

Cause: Mom wants to make molasses oatmeal cookies but has no more molasses.

Effect: ______________________

Effect: The cookie dough becomes sweet and tasty.

Cause: ______________________

Effect: ______________________

Cause: Mom leaves the cookies in the oven too long.

Cause: ______________________

Effect: You get a stomachache.

Photograph ©1985 by Jill Krementz

Name ______________________________

What Is Molasses?

Read this description of molasses. Then answer the questions in complete sentences.

Molasses is a thick brown syrup made from sugar cane. It is used in making candy and baked goods. Farmers also use molasses as food for livestock.

Sugar cane is a tall grass that grows in warm places such as Florida, Cuba, and Hawaii. The plants can be as much as fifteen feet high. Their long stalks contain a sweet juice.

To make sugar, the juice of the sugar cane is boiled several times. After being heated and reheated, the juice forms sugar crystals, but there is still some juice left over. That juice is called *molasses*.

1. What are the uses of molasses? ______________________________

____

2. What plant is molasses made from? ______________________________

____

3. Where does this plant grow? ______________________________

____

4. How is the juice of this plant turned into molasses? ______________________________

____

____

____

Name ______________________________

A Sticky Situation

Each numbered word has a synonym hidden in the puzzle. The words can be read from top to bottom, from left to right, or diagonally. Circle each synonym, and write it in the blanks.

1. sugary ___ ___ ___ ___ ___
2. surprised ___ ___ ___ ___ ___ ___
3. mad ___ ___ ___ ___ ___
4. thin ___ ___ ___ ___ ___ ___
5. impolite ___ ___ ___ ___
6. small ___ ___ ___ ___ ___ ___
7. beneath ___ ___ ___ ___ ___
8. cut ___ ___ ___ ___ ___

W	A	M	E	T	B	K	G	V
A	N	G	R	Y	O	F	S	B
L	A	N	C	D	S	W	L	E
D	R	M	P	U	L	B	I	L
I	R	Q	A	V	I	S	T	O
C	O	F	D	Z	C	J	T	W
S	W	E	E	T	E	M	L	S
B	J	I	G	R	U	D	E	U

Name ________________________________

Dinner Is Served!

Complete the menu by filling in the blanks.

barrels	brag	sweetened	craving
fondness	gooey	slurped	
molasses	pitcher	rumbling	

MENU

MAIN COURSES

Monster Turkey Sandwich **$4.25**

No matter how hungry you are, this dish will satisfy your ________________.

Jumbo Chef's Salad **$4.75**

If you have a ________________ for salad and your stomach is ________________, this is for you!

SIDE DISHES

French Fries **$1.00**

We don't like to ________________, but these are the best.

Pickles **$1.50**

The best pickles are those from our own private ________________.

MENU

DESSERT

Better-Than-Sugar Cake **$4.75**

This is even better than cake ________________ with sugar. It's made from pure ________________.

Ice Cream Sundae **$2.25**

If you have ever had our ________________ fudge sauce, we're sure you ________________ it up!

DRINKS

Soda glass **$ .75**

________________ **$2.50**

Name some foods you'd like to see added to this menu. ________________

____

____

Name

Sticky Stuff

The Vowel + *r* Sounds in *first* Each Spelling Word has the vowel + ***r*** sounds that you hear in ***first.*** These sounds are written as |**û**r|. They can be spelled with the pattern ***er, ir, ur,*** or ***or.***

|ûr| were first turn work

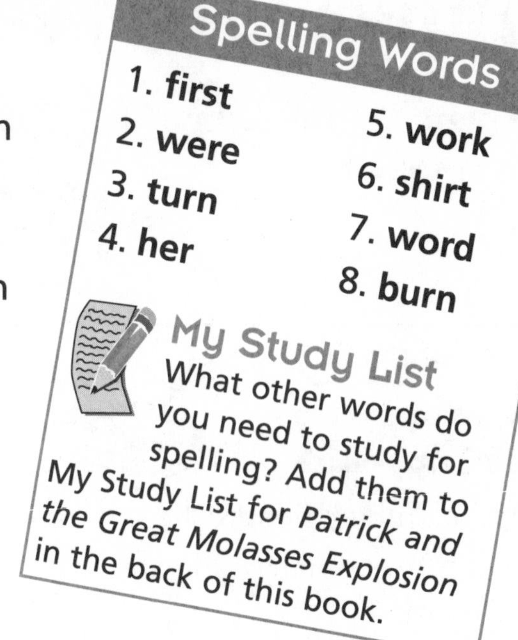

Spelling Words

1. **first**
2. **were**
3. **turn**
4. **her**
5. **work**
6. **shirt**
7. **word**
8. **burn**

My Study List
What other words do you need to study for spelling? Add them to My Study List for *Patrick and the Great Molasses Explosion* in the back of this book.

Help people find what they lost in the molasses! Write each Spelling Word on the item that has the matching spelling for the |ûr| sounds.

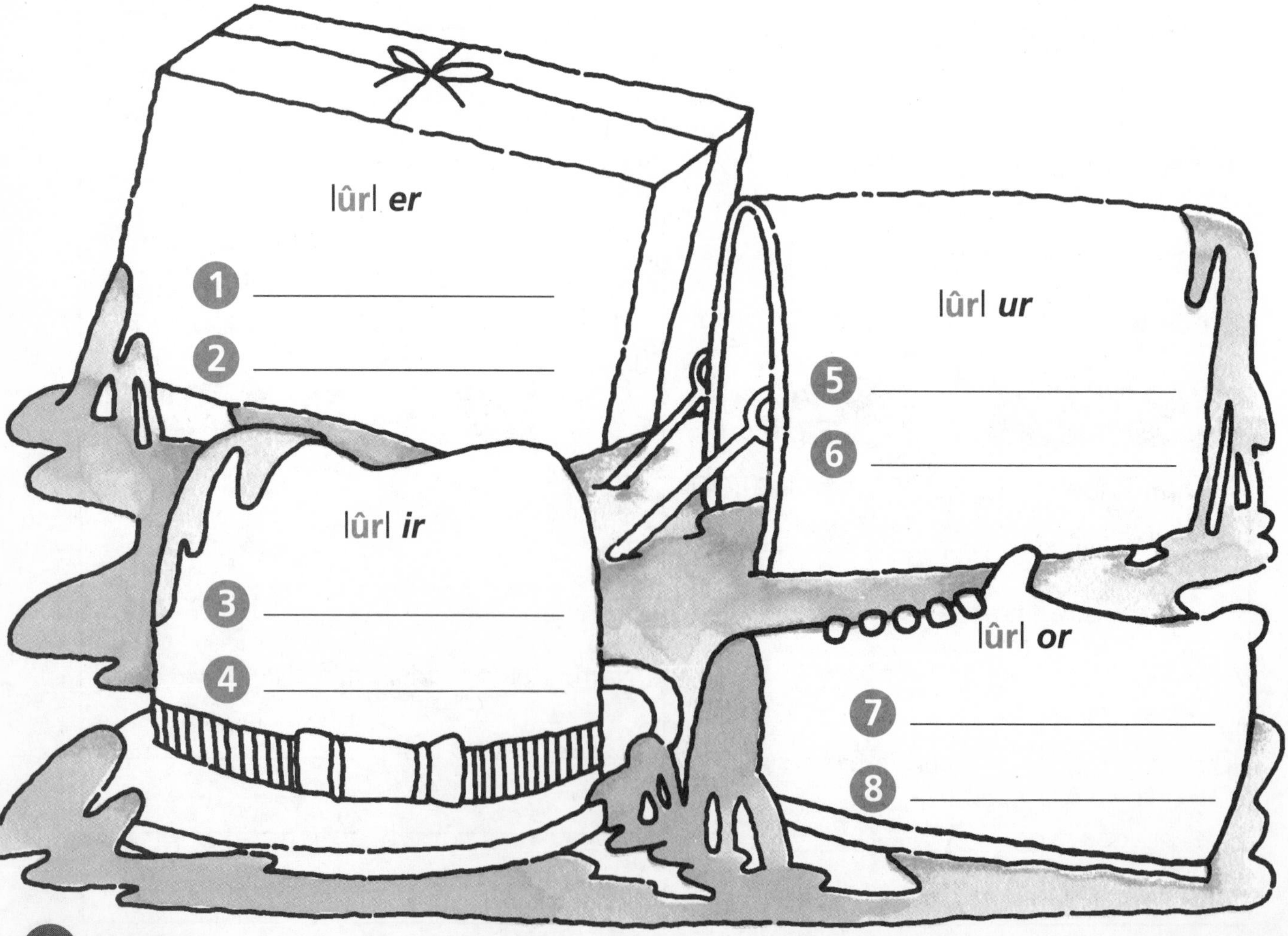

|ûr| *er*

1 ____________

2 ____________

|ûr| *ur*

5 ____________

6 ____________

|ûr| *ir*

3 ____________

4 ____________

|ûr| *or*

7 ____________

8 ____________

Name

Spelling Spree

Proofreading Find and circle four misspelled Spelling Words in this girl's story about the explosion. Then write each word correctly.

Spelling Words

1. first
2. were
3. turn
4. her
5. work
6. shirt
7. word
8. burn

Mother and I wer hanging up the wash in the backyard. First came a boom and then a wave of molasses. Down went the clothesline! Mother's shert was covered with sticky molasses. So was hir hair. Mother was so surprised that she couldn't say a wurd!

1 ____________________

2 ____________________

3 ____________________

4 ____________________

I Was There! Write a Spelling Word to complete each statement about the molasses explosion.

I saw a building catch fire and __(5)__.

I was the __(7)__ person to call the police.

I was on my way to __(6)__ when the explosion happened.

I couldn't __(8)__ my horse in time. He got stuck!

5 ____________________

6 ____________________

7 ____________________

8 ____________________

Many Thanks Patrick never got to thank the man who saved him. Imagine that someone has just saved you. On a separate sheet of paper, write a short letter to thank that person. Use Spelling Words from the list.

Name

"Be" Tankful

The Verb *be* Help

Patrick get the molasses out of the tank. Cross off each verb on the tank when you use it to complete a sentence. When you have used all the words, the tank will be empty.

Subject	Present	Past
I	am	was
you	are	were
he, she, it, singular noun	is	was
we, they	are	were
plural noun	are	were

1. The tank __________ full of sticky molasses. (am, is)
2. I __________ afraid of an accident. (am, are)
3. You __________ also hungry for molasses cookies. (was, were)
4. The workers on the dock __________ heroes. (am, are)
5. We __________ in shock over the molasses flood. (was, were)
6. I __________ late for school again. (was, were)
7. It __________ everywhere. (was, were)
8. The horses __________ upset by this accident. (was, were)
9. You __________ a brave young man. (are, is)
10. They __________ sick of molasses. (are, is)

Name

Beautiful Molassesland

Study the map of a country called Molassesland. Complete the answers to the questions. Use the correct form of *be*.

am
is
are
was
were

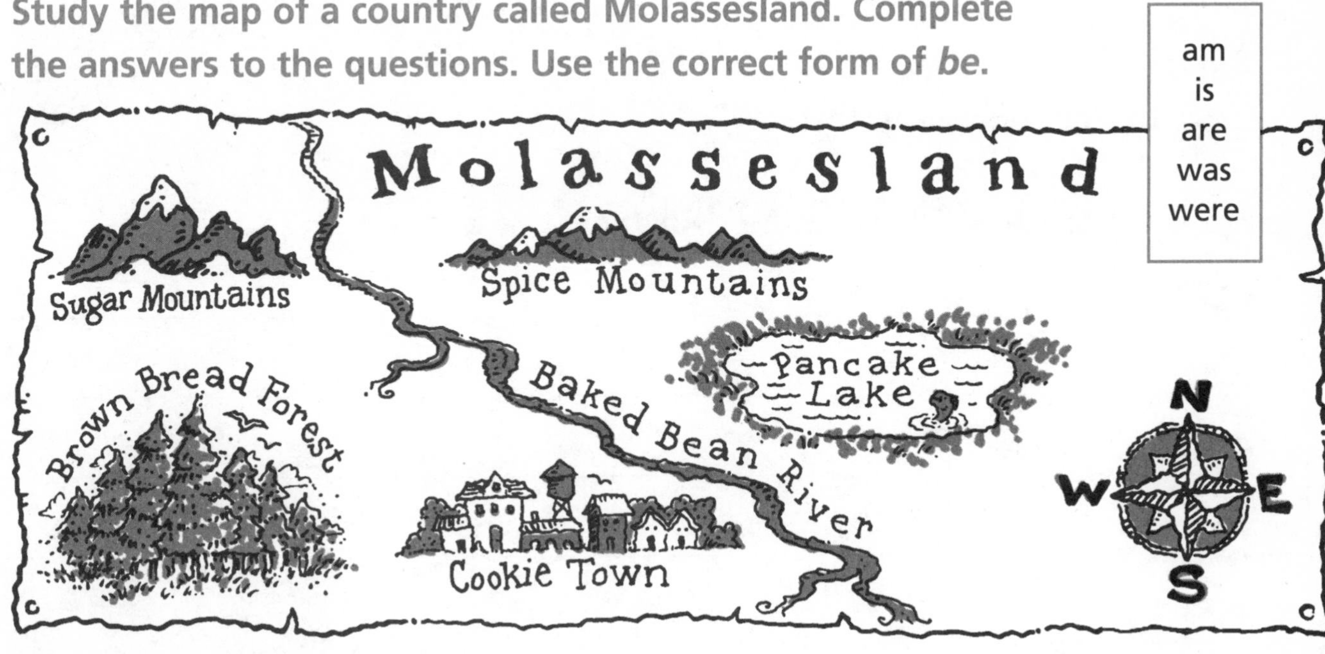

1. What country is this?

   This country ______________________________.

2. What mountains are west of the Spice Mountains?

   Those mountains ______________________________.

3. What is the name of the lake?

   The lake ______________________________.

4. Is Cookie Town east or west of the river?

   Cookie Town ______________________________.

5. Are you sure you have never been to Molassesland?

   I ______________________________.

On a separate sheet of paper, write five sentences about a trip to Molassesland. Use *was* and *were*.

Name ______________________________

A Letter to the Captain

Write to the captain of the *Titanic*. Tell him what he should have done to prevent the disaster. Fill out the chart to help plan your letter.

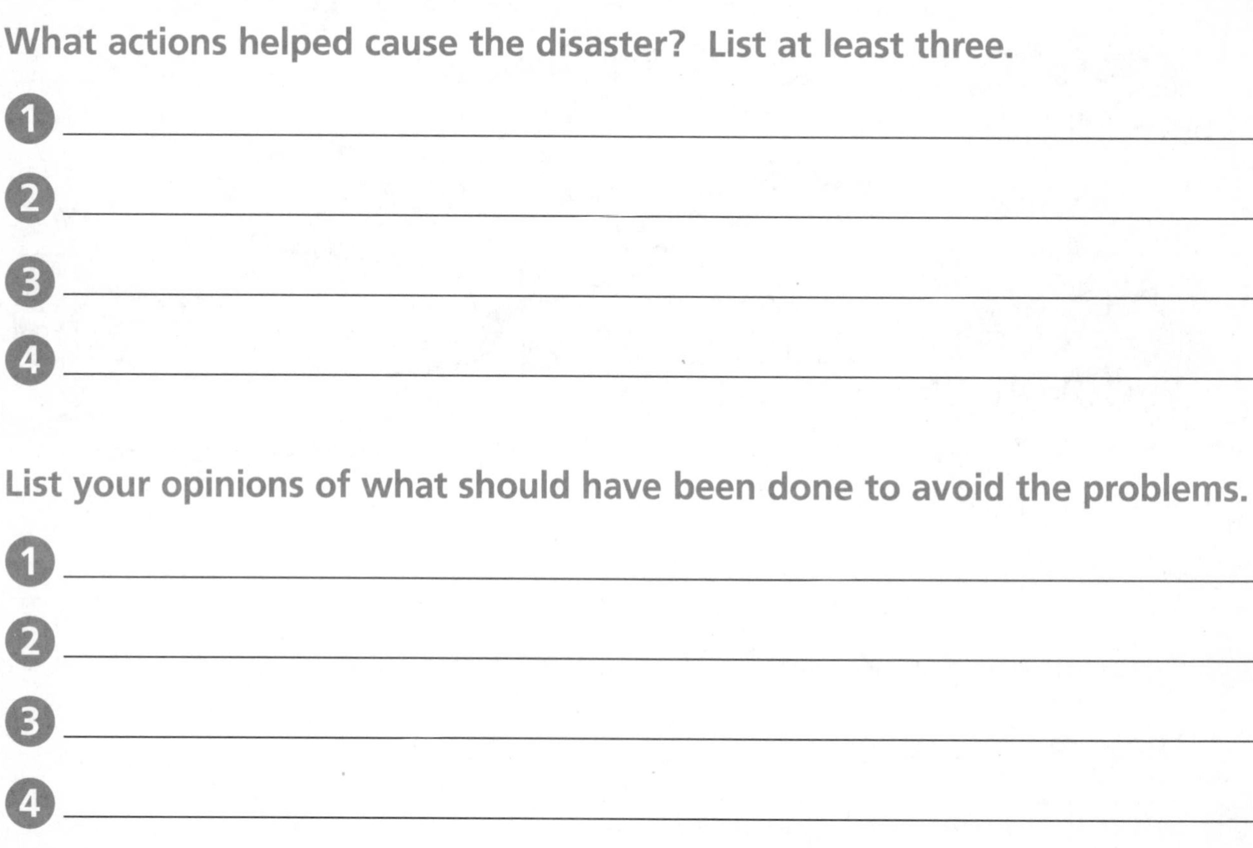

What actions helped cause the disaster? List at least three.

1. ______________________________
2. ______________________________
3. ______________________________
4. ______________________________

List your opinions of what should have been done to avoid the problems.

1. ______________________________
2. ______________________________
3. ______________________________
4. ______________________________

Use the information you listed to write your letter to the captain. Present your work to your class or group. Use the checklist to make sure that you are ready to share your letter.

Checklist

- ☐ My letter shows that I understand the *Titanic* disaster.
- ☐ My letter gives facts about three actions that helped cause the disaster.
- ☐ My letter gives my opinions about what should have been done to prevent the disaster.

STUDENT HANDBOOK

STUDENT HANDBOOK

Contents

Use this log to record the books or other materials you read on your own.

Date

Author

Title

Notes and Comments

Date

Author

Title

Notes and Comments

Date

Author

Title

Notes and Comments

Date

Author

Title

Notes and Comments

Date

Author

Title

Notes and Comments

Date

Author

Title

Notes and Comments

Date

Author

Title

Notes and Comments

Date

Author

Title

Notes and Comments

Date

Author

Title

Notes and Comments

Date

Author

Title

Notes and Comments

Date

Author

Title

Notes and Comments

How to Study a Word

1 LOOK at the word.

- What does the word mean?
- What letters are in the word?
- Name and touch each letter.

2 SAY the word.

- Listen for the consonant sounds.
- Listen for the vowel sounds.

3 THINK about the word.

- How is each sound spelled?
- Close your eyes and picture the word.
- What familiar spelling patterns do you see?
- What other words have the same spelling patterns?

4 WRITE the word.

- Think about the sounds and the letters.
- Form the letters correctly.

5 CHECK the spelling.

- Did you spell the word the same way it is spelled in your word list?
- If you did not spell the word correctly, write the word again.

WORDS OFTEN MISSPELLED

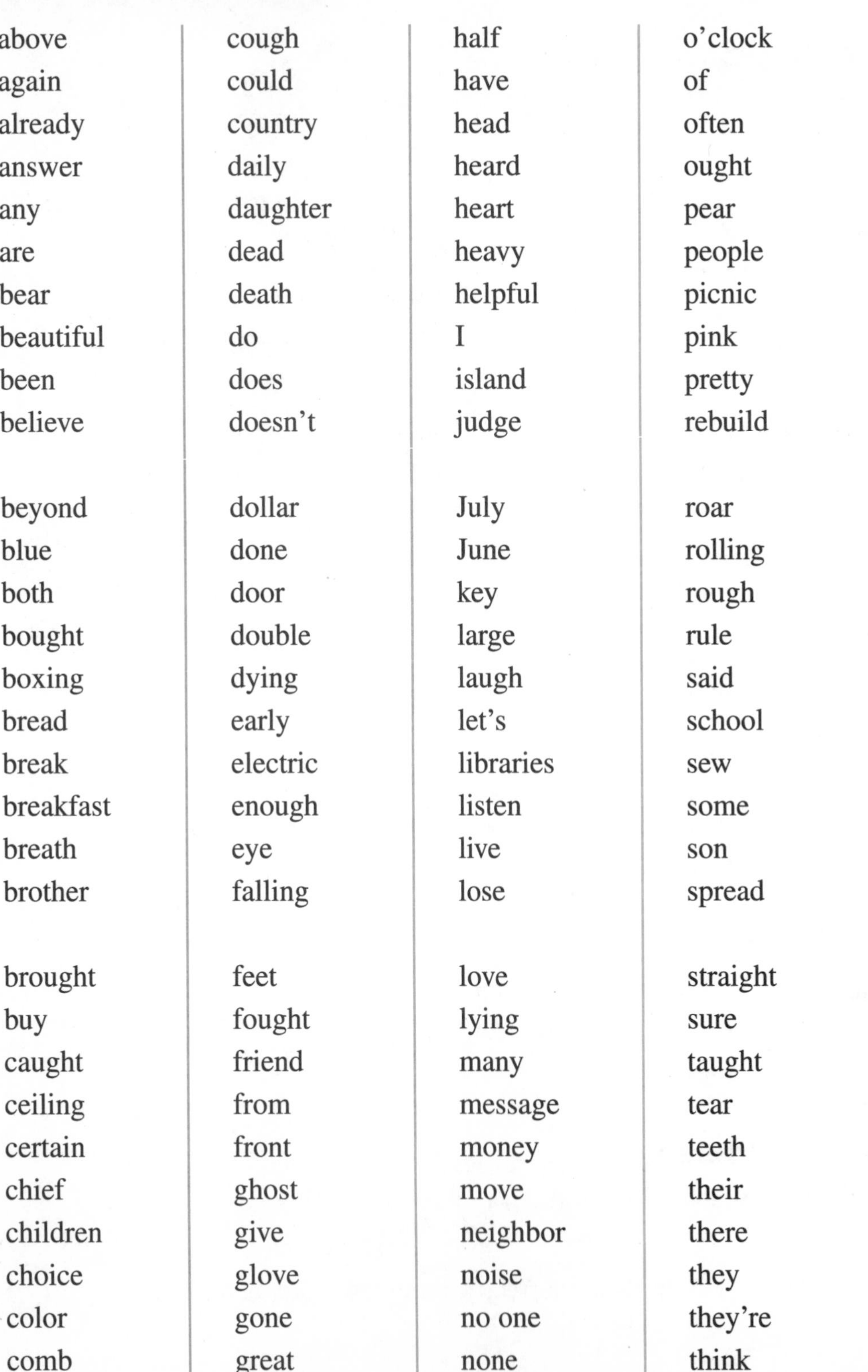

above
again
already
answer
any
are
bear
beautiful
been
believe

beyond
blue
both
bought
boxing
bread
break
breakfast
breath
brother

brought
buy
caught
ceiling
certain
chief
children
choice
color
comb
come

cough
could
country
daily
daughter
dead
death
do
does
doesn't

dollar
done
door
double
dying
early
electric
enough
eye
falling

feet
fought
friend
from
front
ghost
give
glove
gone
great
guess

half
have
head
heard
heart
heavy
helpful
I
island
judge

July
June
key
large
laugh
let's
libraries
listen
live
lose

love
lying
many
message
money
move
neighbor
noise
no one
none
nothing

o'clock
of
often
ought
pear
people
picnic
pink
pretty
rebuild

roar
rolling
rough
rule
said
school
sew
some
son
spread

straight
sure
taught
tear
teeth
their
there
they
they're
think
though

thought
through
to
toe
too
touch
traveling
trouble
two
until

unusual
voice
want
warm
was
wash
watch
weigh
what
where

who
woman
won
wonderful
won't
word
work
worried
you
young
your

Take-Home Word Lists

The Three Little Hawaiian Pigs and the Magic Shark

Spelling Long *a* and Long *e*

/ā/ → t**ai**l, pl**ay**

/ē/ → b**ea**ch, thr**ee**

Spelling Words

1. three
2. tail
3. beach
4. play
5. deep
6. away
7. please
8. chain

Challenge Words

1. easy
2. really
3. reef
4. creature

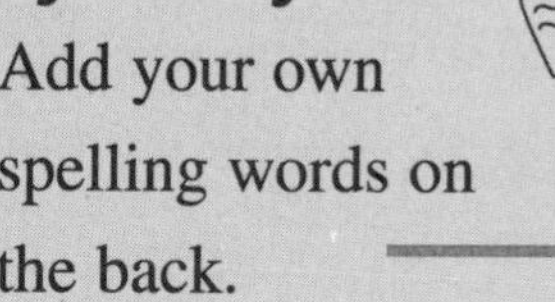

My Study List

Add your own spelling words on the back. →

Take-Home Word Lists

The Three Little Javelinas

Vowel-Consonant-e

/ā/ → sh**ade**

/ē/ → th**ese**

/ī/ → m**ice**

/ō/ → n**ose**

/o͞o/ or /yo͞o/ → **use**

Spelling Words

1. nose
2. these
3. shade
4. use
5. mice
6. smoke
7. snake
8. ripe

Challenge Words

1. escape
2. amaze
3. arrive
4. fortune

My Study List

Add your own spelling words on the back. →

Take-Home Word Lists

The Three Little Wolves and the Big, Bad Pig

Short Vowels

/ă/ → **a**sk

/ĕ/ → n**e**xt

/ĭ/ → m**i**x

/ŏ/ → l**o**ck

/ŭ/ → sh**u**t

Spelling Words

1. ask
2. next
3. mix
4. smell
5. black
6. shut
7. lock
8. truck

Challenge Words

1. knock
2. scent
3. plenty
4. fetch

My Study List

Add your own spelling words on the back. →

Spelling and Writing Word Lists

Name ____________________

My Study List

1. ____________________
2. ____________________
3. ____________________
4. ____________________
5. ____________________
6. ____________________
7. ____________________
8. ____________________
9. ____________________
10. ____________________

Selection Vocabulary

You may want to use these words in your own writing.

1. prowling
2. grunted
3. crumbled
4. trembling
5. scorched

How to Study a Word

LOOK at the word.
SAY the word.
THINK about the word.
WRITE the word.
CHECK the spelling.

Spelling and Writing Word Lists

Name ____________________

My Study List

1. ____________________
2. ____________________
3. ____________________
4. ____________________
5. ____________________
6. ____________________
7. ____________________
8. ____________________
9. ____________________
10. ____________________

Selection Vocabulary

You may want to use these words in your own writing.

1. desert
2. dust storm
3. whirlwind
4. tumbleweeds
5. cactus
6. adobe

How to Study a Word

LOOK at the word.
SAY the word.
THINK about the word.
WRITE the word.
CHECK the spelling.

Spelling and Writing Word Lists

Name ____________________

My Study List

1. ____________________
2. ____________________
3. ____________________
4. ____________________
5. ____________________
6. ____________________
7. ____________________
8. ____________________
9. ____________________
10. ____________________

Selection Vocabulary

You may want to use these words in your own writing.

1. craving
2. anxiously
3. plot
4. scheme
5. pangs
6. furious

How to Study a Word

LOOK at the word.
SAY the word.
THINK about the word.
WRITE the word.
CHECK the spelling.

Take-Home Word Lists

When Jo Louis Won the Title

The Vowel Sounds in *town* and *boy*

|ou| → **tow**n, pr**ou**d
|oi| → n**oi**se, b**oy**

Spelling Words

1. town
2. boy
3. proud
4. crowd
5. noise
6. round
7. voice
8. toy

Challenge Words

1. mountain
2. enjoy
3. annoy
4. thousand

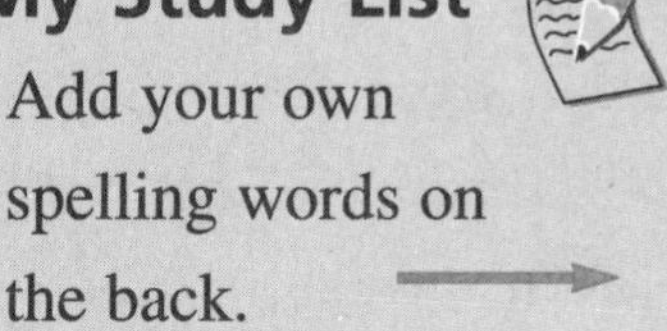

My Study List
Add your own spelling words on the back. →

Take-Home Word Lists

Family Pictures

The Vowel Sounds in *cook* and *knew*

|o͝o| → c**oo**k, p**u**t
|o͞o| → kn**ew**, b**oo**th

Spelling Words

1. cook
2. knew
3. put
4. woods
5. pull
6. booth
7. coop
8. drew

Challenge Words

1. neighborhood
2. afternoon
3. balloon
4. crooked

My Study List
Add your own spelling words on the back. →

Take-Home Word Lists

A Fruit and Vegetable Man

Spelling Long *i* and Long *o*

|ī| → r**igh**t, t**ie**
|ō| → s**oa**p, **ow**n

Spelling Words

1. own
2. right
3. own
4. might
5. tie
6. soap
7. pie
8. float

Challenge Words

1. sigh
2. flown
3. delight
4. follow

My Study List
Add your own spelling words on the back. →

Name ______________________

My Study List

1. ______________________
2. ______________________
3. ______________________
4. ______________________
5. ______________________
6. ______________________
7. ______________________
8. ______________________
9. ______________________
10. ______________________

Selection Vocabulary

You may want to use these words in your own writing.

1. market
2. pyramids
3. diamonds
4. accent
5. designs
6. triangles

How to Study a Word

LOOK at the word.
SAY the word.
THINK about the word.
WRITE the word.
CHECK the spelling.

Spelling and Writing Word Lists

Name ______________________

My Study List

1. ______________________
2. ______________________
3. ______________________
4. ______________________
5. ______________________
6. ______________________
7. ______________________
8. ______________________
9. ______________________
10. ______________________

Selection Vocabulary

You may want to use these words in your own writing.

1. recognize
2. scene
3. custom
4. inspired

How to Study a Word

LOOK at the word.
SAY the word.
THINK about the word.
WRITE the word.
CHECK the spelling.

136

Spelling and Writing Word Lists

Name ______________________

My Study List

1. ______________________
2. ______________________
3. ______________________
4. ______________________
5. ______________________
6. ______________________
7. ______________________
8. ______________________
9. ______________________
10. ______________________

Selection Vocabulary

You may want to use these words in your own writing.

1. whirled
2. tattered
3. bellowed
4. title fight
5. title
6. braced

How to Study a Word

LOOK at the word.
SAY the word.
THINK about the word.
WRITE the word.
CHECK the spelling.

136

Patrick and the Great Molasses Explosion

The Vowel + *r* Sounds in *first*

/ûr/ → w**er**e, f**ir**st, t**ur**n, w**or**k

Spelling Words

1. first
2. were
3. turn
4. her
5. work
6. shirt
7. word
8. burn

Challenge Words

1. stern
2. hurry
3. perfect
4. thorough

My Study List

Add your own spelling words on the back. →

Take-Home Word Lists

Pompeii...Buried Alive!

Vowels + *r* Sounds

/är/ → d**ar**k
/îr/ → n**ear**
/ôr/ → st**or**y, m**ore**

Spelling Words

1. dark
2. more
3. start
4. story
5. near
6. morning
7. part
8. year

Challenge Words

1. horrible
2. enormous
3. explore
4. argue

My Study List

Add your own spelling words on the back. →

137

Take-Home Word Lists

The Titanic: Lost...And Found

The Vowel Sound in *saw*

/ô/ → s**aw**, t**al**k, th**ough**t, c**augh**t

Spelling Words

1. saw
2. talk
3. small
4. thought
5. law
6. caught
7. fought
8. taught

Challenge Words

1. already
2. flaw
3. although
4. daughter

My Study List

Add your own spelling words on the back. →

137

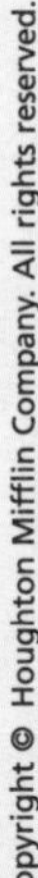

Spelling and Writing Word Lists

Name ____________________

My Study List

1. ____________________
2. ____________________
3. ____________________
4. ____________________
5. ____________________
6. ____________________
7. ____________________
8. ____________________
9. ____________________
10. ____________________

Selection Vocabulary

You may want to use these words in your own writing.

1. passengers
2. voyage
3. orders
4. rescue
5. survivors

How to Study a Word

LOOK at the word.
SAY the word.
THINK about the word.
WRITE the word.
CHECK the spelling.

Spelling and Writing Word Lists

Name ____________________

My Study List

1. ____________________
2. ____________________
3. ____________________
4. ____________________
5. ____________________
6. ____________________
7. ____________________
8. ____________________
9. ____________________
10. ____________________

Selection Vocabulary

You may want to use these words in your own writing.

1. volcano
2. erupted
3. gas
4. poisonous
5. tremble
6. buried

How to Study a Word

LOOK at the word.
SAY the word.
THINK about the word.
WRITE the word.
CHECK the spelling.

Spelling and Writing Word Lists

Name ____________________

My Study List

1. ____________________
2. ____________________
3. ____________________
4. ____________________
5. ____________________
6. ____________________
7. ____________________
8. ____________________
9. ____________________
10. ____________________

Selection Vocabulary

You may want to use these words in your own writing.

1. molasses
2. gooey
3. barrels
4. pitcher

How to Study a Word

LOOK at the word.
SAY the word.
THINK about the word.
WRITE the word.
CHECK the spelling.

SPELLING GUIDELINES

1 Short Vowel Patterns

A short vowel sound is usually spelled *a, e, i, o,* or *u* and is followed by a consonant sound.	ask next mix	lock shut

2 Long Vowel Sounds

The long *a* sound can be spelled with the pattern *a*-consonant-*e*, *ai,* or *ay*.	shade tail	play
The long *e* sound is often spelled with the pattern *e*-consonant-*e*, *ea,* or *ee*.	these beach	deep
The long *i* sound can be spelled with the pattern *i*-consonant-*e*, *igh,* or *ie*.	ripe right	tie
The long *o* sound can be spelled with the pattern *o*-consonant-*e*, *oa,* or *ow*.	home soap	own
The long *u* sound /yōō/ or /ōō/ may be spelled with the pattern *u*-consonant-*e*, *ew,* or *oo*.	use drew	booth
The long *i* sound at the end of a word may be spelled *y*.	cry	
The long *e* sound at the end of a word may be spelled *y*.	penny	

3 Other Vowel Sounds

The vowel sound in *cook* may be spelled with the pattern *oo* or *u*.	woods	pull
The sound /ou/ is often spelled with the pattern *ow* or *ou*.	town	proud
The sound /oi/ is spelled with the pattern *oi* or *oy*.	noise	boy
The vowel sound in *saw* can be spelled with the pattern *aw*, *a* before *l*, *ough*, or *augh*.	saw talk	thought caught

4 Vowel + *r* Sounds

The vowel + *r* sounds you hear in *dark* can be spelled with the pattern *ar*.	start	
The vowel + *r* sounds you hear in *near* can be spelled with the pattern *ear*.	year	
The vowel + *r* sounds you hear in *more* can be spelled with the patterns *or* and *ore*.	story	store
The vowel + *r* sounds in *first* can be spelled with the pattern *er*, *ir*, *ur,* or *or*.	were first	turn work

SPELLING GUIDELINES

5 Consonant Sounds

The /s/ sound you hear at the beginning of *city* may be spelled *c* when the *c* is followed by *i* or *e*.	**ci**rcle	on**ce**
The /j/ sound you hear at the beginning of *just* can be spelled with the consonant *j* or with the consonant *g* followed by *e*.	**j**ust	lar**ge**

6 Syllable Patterns

The schwa + *r* sounds that you hear in *grandmother* are often spelled with the pattern *er*.	nev**er**	
The schwa + *l* sounds that you hear in *people* can be spelled with the pattern *le*.	tab**le**	
Some two-syllable words have the vowel-consonant-consonant-vowel pattern (VCCV). Divide a word with this pattern between the two consonants to find the syllables. Look for spelling patterns you have learned. Spell the word by syllables.	win/ dow	din/ ner

7 Word Endings

Add *s* to most words to name more than one. Add *es* to words that end with *s*, *x*, *sh*, or *ch* to name more than one.	trip**s** bus**es** box**es**	wish**es** peach**es**
If a base word ends with *e*, drop the *e* before adding the ending *-ed* or *-ing*.	shap**e** - shap**ed** tak**e** - tak**ing**	
If a base word ends with a vowel and a single consonant, double the consonant before adding *-ed* or *-ing*.	drop**ped**	hit**ting**
When a base word ends with a consonant and *y*, change the *y* to *i* before adding *-es* or *-ed*.	sky - sk**ies** try - tr**ied**	

8 Prefixes and Suffixes

Prefixes are added to the beginning of base words or word roots. *Re-*, *un-*, and *dis-* are prefixes.	**re**read **un**fair	**dis**like
Suffixes are added to the end of base words or word roots.These word parts are suffixes: *-ful*, *-ly*, *-er*.	play**ful** soft**ly**	writ**er**

9 Homophones and Contractions See Problem Words, p. 160.

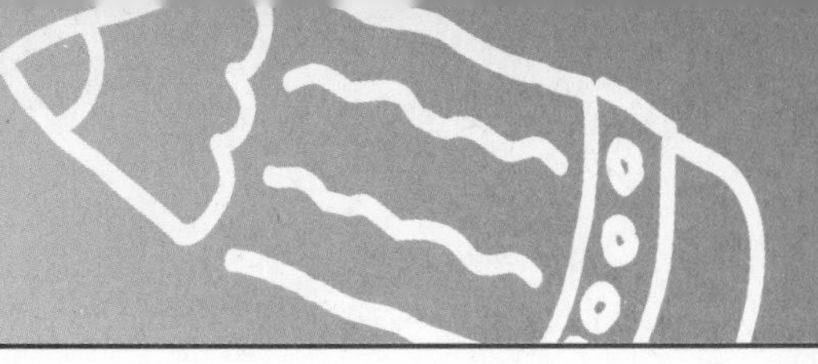

A Resource for Grammar, Usage, Punctuation, and Capitalization

SENTENCES

Definition

A **sentence** is a group of words that tells a complete thought. It tells who or what, and it tells what happens. A sentence begins with a capital letter.

Lightning flashed in the sky. **T**he forest ranger spotted fire.

- A group of words is not a sentence unless it has both parts—the part that tells who or what and the part that tells what happens. These examples are NOT sentences.

  Flashed in the sky. During the storm. When the tree fell.

Kinds of Sentences

There are four kinds of sentences.

- A **statement** is a sentence that tells something. It ends with a period.

  Deserts are dry**.**

- A **question** is a sentence that asks something. It ends with a question mark.

  Do you like deserts**?**

- A **command** is a sentence that tells someone to do something. It ends with a period.

  Always carry water**.**

- An **exclamation** shows strong feeling. It ends with an exclamation point (**!**).

  How hot it was**!** It was so hot**!**

Subjects and Predicates

Every sentence has a **subject** and a **predicate.**

- The **subject** tells whom or what the sentence is about.

  Captain Ortega is a good pilot. **The large jet** carries many people.

- The **predicate** is the part of a sentence that tells what the subject does or is.

  Captain Ortega **is a good pilot.** The large jet **carries many people.**

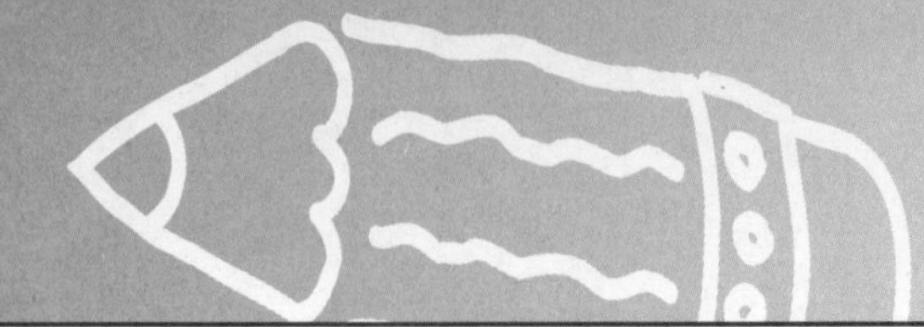

Run-on Sentences

A **run-on sentence** is two or more sentences that are run together incorrectly. Do not run sentences together.

- Correct a run-on sentence by adding end marks and capital letters to separate each complete thought.

Run-on: Electricians often wear rubber gloves electricity cannot go through rubber.

Corrected: Electricians often wear rubber gloves**.** **E**lectricity cannot go through rubber.

NOUNS

Definition

A **noun** names a person, a place, or a thing.

Nouns		
Persons	boy student	writer Li Chen
Places	lake Fenway Park	Olympia mountain
Things	boat calendar	sweater *Little Women*

Common and Proper Nouns

A **common noun** names any person, place, or thing.

doctor country holiday

A **proper noun** names a particular person, place, or thing. Proper nouns begin with capital letters. A proper noun, like *Pine Lake*, may have more than one word. Begin each important word in a proper noun with a capital letter.

Dr. Juarez Sudan Fourth of July

Common Nouns	Proper Nouns
My **friend** swam today. Her **dog** went with her. The **lake** was cold.	**Suzy** swam today. **Buddy** went with her. **Pine Lake** was cold.

Singular and Plural Nouns

Singular nouns name one person, place, or thing.

Julie climbed a tree. She played on a swing.

Plural nouns name more than one person, place, or thing.

Julie climbed two trees. She played on some swings.

- Form the plural of most nouns by adding *s* or *es* to the singular. Look at the ending of the singular noun to help you decide on whether to add *s* or *es* to form the plural.

Rules for Forming Plural Nouns		
1. Most singular nouns: Add *s*	street house	street**s** house**s**
2. Nouns ending in *s*, *sh*, *ch*, or *x*: Add *es*.	dress dish bench ax	dress**es** dish**es** bench**es** ax**es**
3. Nouns ending with a consonant and *y*: Change the *y* to *i* and add *es*.	city cranberry	cit**ies** cranberr**ies**
4. Nouns that have special plural spelling.	woman mouse foot ox	wom**e**n m**ice** f**ee**t ox**en**

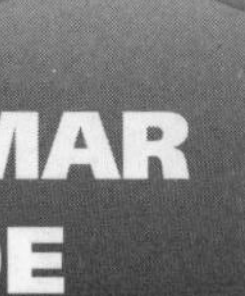

GRAMMAR GUIDE

Singular and Plural Possessive Nouns

A **possessive noun** shows ownership. Possessive nouns can be singular or plural. When a possessive noun is singular, it shows that one person, place, or thing has or owns something.

- To form the possessive of a singular noun, add an apostrophe (**'**) and *s*.

Singular Nouns	Singular Possessive Nouns
boy	boy**'s** bike
Amy	Amy**'s** game
cat	cat**'s** paws

When a possessive noun is plural, it shows that more than one person, place, or thing has or owns something.

- If a plural noun ends with *s,* add only an apostrophe.

Plural Nouns	Plural Possessive Nouns
teams	two teams**'** bats
bunnies	bunnies**'** carrots
classes	classes**'** books

VERBS

Definition

A **verb** is a word that shows action. The verb is the main word in the predicate.

The fire **burns** brightly. It **lasts** for hours.

Helping Verbs

Has and *have* are **helping verbs.** They help other verbs to show past time.

- Use *has* with a singular noun in the subject and with *he, she,* or *it*.

  Ada **has** played the game. She **has** enjoyed it.

- Use *have* with a plural noun in the subject and with *I, you, we,* or *they.*

  The boys **have** helped her. I **have** watched.

The Verb *be*

The verb *be* does not show action. It tells what someone or something is or was.

- The verb *be* has special forms.

  I **am** in fifth grade.
  You **are** younger.
  Mr. Roberts **is** my teacher.
  I **was** late for school today.
  The other students **were** already inside.

- *Am, is,* and *are* show present time.

  I **am** sleepy now.
  It **is** a four-hour drive.
  Today we **are** in Maine.

- *Was* and *were* show past time.

  It **was** a long trip. Friday we **were** in Vermont.

Subject	Present	Past
I	am	was
you	are	were
he, she, it	is	was
singular noun (John)	is	was
we	are	were
they	are	were
plural noun (dogs)	are	were

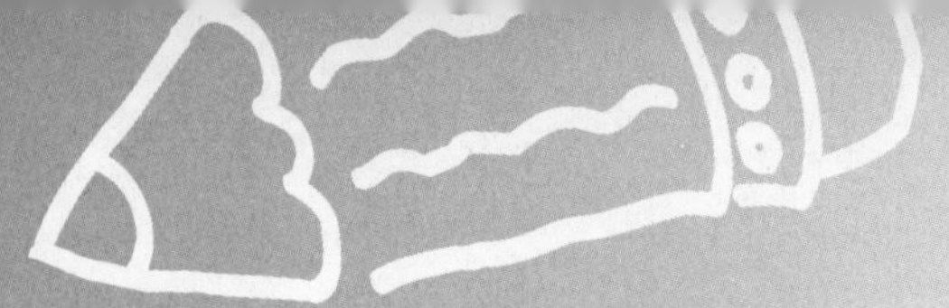

GRAMMAR GUIDE

Verbs in the Present

Verbs show action in sentences. Verbs also tell when the action happens.

A **verb in present time** tells what is happening now. The form of a verb in present time depends on its subject.

- Add *s* to a verb in the present when the noun in the subject is singular.

  The **dog** barks at the snowman. **Jill** laughs.

- Do not add *s* to a verb in the present when the noun in the subject is plural.

  The boys **shovel**. Their parents **start** the car.

- Add *es* to a verb that ends with *s, sh, ch,* or *x* when it is used with a singular noun.

  The **broom** brushes the snow off the porch.

- If a verb ends with a consonant and *y,* change the *y* to *i* before adding *es.*

  A neighbor carr**ies** the shovel to the car.

Singular	Plural
Rob **tosses** a ball.	The boys **toss** the ball.
My grandfather **fishes**.	The girls **fish**.
Mother **watches** us.	People **watch** us.
Emily **mixes** the salad.	Friends **mix** the salad.

GRAMMAR GUIDE

Verbs in the Past

A **verb in past time** shows that an action has already happened.

- Add *-ed* to most verbs to show past time.

  We **cooked** our dinner over a campfire. It **begged** for a peanut.
  A squirrel **hoped** for a few crumbs. Then the squirrel **hurried** away.

The spelling of some verbs changes when you add *-ed.*

- When a verb ends in *e*, drop the *e* before adding *-ed.*

  race - **e** + **ed** = race**d** joke - **e** + **ed** = joke**d**

- When a verb ends with a consonant and *y,* change the *y* to *i* and add *-ed.*

  stud**y** - **y** + **i** + **ed** = stud**ied** hurr**y** - **y** + **i** + **ed** = hurr**ied**

- When a verb ends with one vowel followed by one consonant, double the final consonant and add *-ed.*

  sto**p** + **p** + **ed** = sto**pped** hu**g** + **g** + **ed** = hu**gged**
  pla**n** + **n** + **ed** = pla**nned** dra**g** + **g** + **ed** = dra**gged**

Irregular Verbs

Some verbs are special: they do not end in *-ed* to show past time. They have one spelling to show past time and another spelling when used with *has, have*, or *had.*

Present: Many people **run** in Boston's big race.
Past: William **ran** in the race last year.
With *has*: Anita **has run** in the race many times.

There are many irregular verbs in the English language. See the chart on the next page.

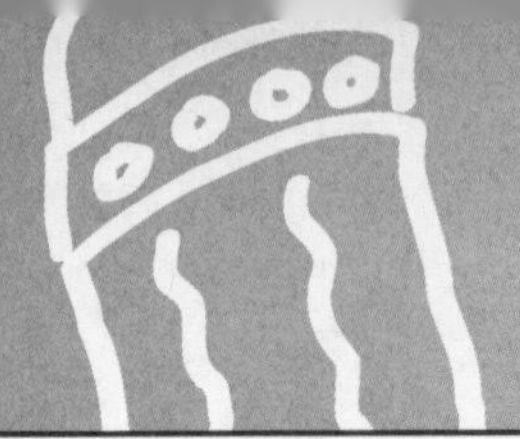

GRAMMAR GUIDE

Irregular Verbs		
Present	**Past**	**Past with *has, have,* or *had***
begin	began	(has, have, had) begun
blow	blew	(has, have, had) blown
break	broke	(has, have, had) broken
bring	brought	(has, have, had) brought
choose	chose	(has, have, had) chosen
come	came	(has, have, had) come
do	did	(has, have, had) done
eat	ate	(has, have, had) eaten
fly	flew	(has, have, had) flown
freeze	froze	(has, have, had) frozen
give	gave	(has, have, had) given
go	went	(has, have, had) gone
grow	grew	(has, have, had) grown
know	knew	(has, have, had) known
make	made	(has, have, had) made
ring	rang	(has, have, had) rung
run	ran	(has, have, had) run
say	said	(has, have, had) said
see	saw	(has, have, had) seen
sing	sang	(has, have, had) sung
speak	spoke	(has, have, had) spoken
steal	stole	(has, have, had) stolen
swim	swam	(has, have, had) swum
take	took	(has, have, had) taken
tear	tore	(has, have, had) torn
think	thought	(has, have, had) thought
wear	wore	(has, have, had) worn
write	wrote	(has, have, had) written

ADJECTIVES

What Are Adjectives?

An **adjective** is a word that describes a noun.

- An adjective may tell *what kind.*

  Loud sirens woke me up. (What kind of sirens?)

  The **old** barn was on fire. (What kind of barn?)

- Adjectives such as *one, ten, many,* and *several* tell *how many.*

  Two families were rescued by firefighters.

  Fire trucks from **many** towns arrived.

- Adjectives usually come before the noun they are describing.

  A **black** dog barked at the trucks.
  Firefighters sprayed water on the **angry** flames.

Articles

A, *an*, and *the* are special adjectives called **articles**. *A* and *an* refer to any person, place, or thing. *The* refers to a particular person, place, or thing.

- Use *a* and *an* before singular nouns.
- Use *the* before singular and plural nouns.

a	Use before a word that begins with a consonant sound.	**a** jet **a** high step
an	Use before a word that begins with a vowel sound.	**an** engineer **an** hour
the	Use before singular and plural words.	**the** plans

Comparing with Adjectives

To compare two people, places, or things, add *-er* to most adjectives.

Mars is a **smaller** planet than Jupiter.

To compare more than two people, places, or things, add *-est*.

Pluto is the **smallest** planet of all.

Adjective	Compare two.	Compare three or more.
Neptune is **warm**.	Uranus is **warmer** than Neptune.	Saturn is the **warmest** of the three.

ADVERBS

What Are Adverbs?

A word that describes a verb is an **adverb**.

- Adverbs tell *how, when*, and *where* an action happens.

Kim walked up to the horse **bravely**. (walked how?)

Next, she sat on the horse. (sat when?)

The horse stood **there**. (stood where?)

- Adverbs that tell *how* usually end in *-ly*.

How		When		Where	
easily	safely	always	soon	ahead	here
certainly	secretly	first	then	around	nearby
fast	slowly	later	today	away	out
happily	softly	next	tomorrow	everywhere	there
quietly	together	often	yesterday	far	upstairs

PRONOUNS

Definition

A **pronoun** takes the place of one or more nouns.

Nouns	Pronouns
Carl watches the swimmers. The swimmers listen for the whistle.	**He** watches the swimmers. **They** listen for the whistle.

Subject Pronouns

The pronouns *I, you, he, she, it, we,* and *they* are **subject pronouns**. Pronouns can be singular or plural.

Subject Pronouns	
Singular	**Plural**
I you he, she, it	we you they

- Use **subject pronouns** as subjects of sentences.

  I will compete in a swimming race. **You** offered some tips.

Use the form of the verb in the present that goes with the subject pronoun.

- Add *s* or *es* to a verb in the present when the subject is *he, she,* or *it.*

  She **fixes** dinner. He **sets** the table.

- Do not add *s* or *es* to a verb in the present when the subject is *I, you, we,* or *they.*

  I **fix** dinner. We **set** the table.

GRAMMAR GUIDE

Object Pronouns

The pronouns *me, you, him, her, it, us,* and *them* are **object pronouns.**

- Object pronouns follow action verbs and words like *to, for, at, of,* and *with.*

Nouns	Pronouns
Nina painted with Lou.	Nina painted with **him**.
Ben and I met Nina and Lou.	Ben and I met **them**.
Ben brought a brush.	Ben brought **it**.

- Object pronouns can be singular or plural.

Object Pronouns	
Singular	**Plural**
me	us
you	you
him, her, it	them

- Use **object pronouns** as objects of sentences.

  Mr. Russell told **us** about the play.
  Lisa tried out for **it.**
  Dale and Kristin made a costume for **you**.
  Joy watched **them** last night.

- *It* and *you* are both subject or object pronouns.

Subject Pronouns	Object Pronouns
It was a big success.	The parents loved **it**.
You came backstage.	The flowers are for **you**.

I and *me*

- Use *I* as the subject of a sentence. Use *me* as an object pronoun. Always capitalize the word *I*.

  Subject Pronoun: **I** left a message for Nat.
  Object Pronoun: Nat called **me** right back.

- Name yourself last when you talk about another person and yourself.

  Nat and I helped Mom. She gave **Nat and me** some money.

- Try this test if you have trouble choosing between *I* and *me*. Say the sentence with only *I* or *me*. Leave out the other noun.

  Nat and I went to the store. **I** went to the store.
  Dad walked with **Nat and me**. Dad walked with **me**.

Possessive Pronouns

A **possessive pronoun** shows ownership. Possessive pronouns can take the place of possessive nouns.

Possessive Nouns	Possessive Pronouns
Amy's radio is broken.	**Her** radio is broken.
She took it to Al's shop.	She took it to **his** shop.
Amy has the twins' radio.	Amy has **their** radio.

The pronouns *my, your, her, his, its, our,* and *their* are possessive pronouns.

My class watches the gorillas.
Their names are Koko and Michael.
Koko wants to shake **your** hand.
Michael waves to **our** teacher.
Her best friend is Michael.
Michael paints a picture on **his** paper.
The gorilla sits on **its** blanket.

ABBREVIATIONS

Abbreviations are shortened forms of words. Most abbreviations begin with a capital letter and end with a period.

• Titles

Mr. *(Mister)* Mr. Pedro Arupe
Mrs. *(Mistress)* Mrs. Jane Chang
Ms. Carla Tower
Sr. *(Senior)* James Morton, Sr.
Jr. *(Junior)* James Morton, Jr.
Dr. *(Doctor)* Dr. Ellen Masters

Note: *Miss* is not an abbreviation and does not end with a period.

• Words used in addresses

St. *(Street)*
Rd. *(Road)*
Blvd. *(Boulevard)*
Ave. *(Avenue)*

• Days of the week

Sun. *(Sunday)*
Mon. *(Monday)*
Tues. *(Tuesday)*
Wed. *(Wednesday)*
Thurs. *(Thursday)*
Fri. *(Friday)*
Sat. *(Saturday)*

• Months of the year

Jan. *(January)*
Feb. *(February)*
Mar. *(March)*
Apr. *(April)*
Aug. *(August)*
Sept. *(September)*
Oct. *(October)*
Nov. *(November)*
Dec. *(December)*

Note: May, June, and July are not abbreviated.

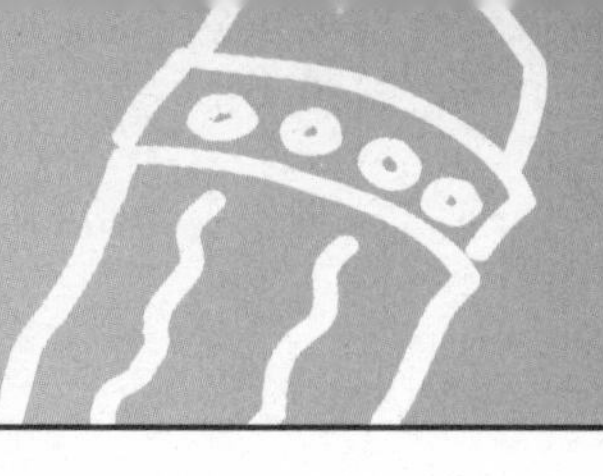

ABBREVIATIONS (continued)

• States

The United States Postal Service uses two capital letters and no period in each of its state abbreviations.

AL *(Alabama)*
AK *(Alaska)*
AZ *(Arizona)*
AR *(Arkansas)*
CA *(California)*
CO *(Colorado)*
CT *(Connecticut)*
DE *(Delaware)*
FL *(Florida)*
GA *(Georgia)*
HI *(Hawaii)*
ID *(Idaho)*
IL *(Illinois)*
IN *(Indiana)*
IA *(Iowa)*
KS *(Kansas)*
KY *(Kentucky)*
LA *(Louisiana)*
ME *(Maine)*
MD *(Maryland)*
MA *(Massachusetts)*
MI *(Michigan)*
MN *(Minnesota)*
MS *(Mississippi)*
MO *(Missouri)*
MT *(Montana)*
NE *(Nebraska)*
NV *(Nevada)*
NH *(New Hampshire)*
NJ *(New Jersey)*
NM *(New Mexico)*
NY *(New York)*
NC *(North Carolina)*
ND *(North Dakota)*
OH *(Ohio)*
OK *(Oklahoma)*
OR *(Oregon)*
PA *(Pennsylvania)*
RI *(Rhode Island)*
SC *(South Carolina)*
SD *(South Dakota)*
TN *(Tennessee)*
TX *(Texas)*
UT *(Utah)*
VT *(Vermont)*
VA *(Virginia)*
WA *(Washington)*
WV *(West Virginia)*
WI *(Wisconsin)*
WY *(Wyoming)*

TITLES

Underlining

Titles of books, newspapers, magazines, and TV series are underlined. The important words and the first and last words are capitalized.

<u>The Call of the Wild</u> <u>Time</u> <u>Nature</u>

Computer Tip: Use italic type for the titles of books and newspapers instead of underlining: *Life on the Mississippi; The New York Times.*

Quotation marks

Put quotation marks *(“ ”)* around the titles of short stories, articles, songs, poems, and book chapters.

“The Red Pony” (short story) “Song of the South” (song)

QUOTATIONS

Quotation marks

A **direct quotation** tells a speaker’s exact words. Use quotation marks *(“ ”)* to set off a direct quotation from the rest of the sentence.

“Please iron your shirt tonight,” said Ms. Hilton.

Begin a quotation with a capital letter. When a quotation comes at the end of a sentence, use a comma to separate the quotation from the words that tell who is speaking. Put end marks inside the last quotation mark.

The principal announced, “The library will be open today.”

Writing a conversation

Begin a new paragraph each time a new person begins speaking.

“Are you going to drive all the way to Columbus in one day?” asked my Uncle Ben.

“I really haven’t decided,” said my father. “I was hoping that you would share the driving with me.”

CAPITALIZATION

Rules for capitalization

Every sentence begins with a capital letter.

What a wonderful day this is!

The pronoun *I* is always a capital letter.

What can I do this afternoon?

Begin each important word in the names of particular persons, pets, places, and things (proper nouns) with a capital letter.

Morris Gulf of Mexico Avery Place Washington Monument

Titles and their abbreviations when used with a person's name begin with a capital letter. Use a capital letter for a person's initials.

Sheriff Tilden Mrs. Garcia Laura B. Hecht Judge Diego

Family titles when they are used as names or as parts of names begin with a capital letter.

We called Aunt Leslie. May we leave now, Grandpa?

Begin the names of days, months, and holidays with a capital letter.

Next Monday is the Fourth of July.

The names of groups begin with a capital letter.

Aspen Mountain Club International League

The first and last words and all important words in the titles of books and newspapers begin with a capital letter. Titles of books and newspapers are underlined.

Secrets of a Wildlife Watcher The Los Angeles Times

GRAMMAR GUIDE

CAPITALIZATION (continued)

The first word in the greeting and the closing of a letter begins with a capital letter.

Dear Melissa, Sincerely yours,

PUNCTUATION

End marks

There are three end marks. A period *(.)* ends a statement or a command. A question mark *(?)* follows a question. An exclamation point *(!)* follows an exclamation.

The notebook is on the shelf. *(statement)*
Watch that program at eight tonight. *(command)*
Where does the trail end? *(question)*
This is your highest score this year! *(exclamation)*

Apostrophe

Add an apostrophe *(')* and *s* to a singular noun to make it show ownership.

day's James's grandfather's community's

For a plural noun ending in *s*, add just an apostrophe *(')* to show ownership.

sisters' families' Smiths' hound dogs'

For a plural noun that does not end in *s*, add an apostrophe *(')* and *s*.

teeth's men's children's

Use an apostrophe in contractions in place of missing letters.

isn't *(is not)*	it's *(it is)*
can't *(cannot)*	I'm *(I am)*
won't *(will not)*	they've *(they have)*
wasn't *(was not)*	they'll *(they will)*
we're *(we are)*	

Comma

A comma (,) tells the reader to pause between the words that it separates.

Use commas to separate a series of three or more words. Put a comma after each item in the series except the last one.

We made a salad of lettuce, peppers, and onions.

You can combine two short, related sentences to make one compound sentence. Use a comma and the connecting word *and, but,* or *or*.

The sky became dark, and we heard thunder.

Use commas after *yes, no, well*, and order words when they begin a sentence.

Yes, it's a perfect day for a picnic.
First, find the basket.
Well, I'll make dessert.
No, the ants will not bother us.

Use a comma or commas to set off the names of people who are spoken to directly.

Gloria, hold this light for me. How was the movie, Grandma?

Use a comma to separate the month and the day from the year.

I was born on July 3, 1988.

Use a comma between the names of a city and a state.

Denver, Colorado Tulsa, Oklahoma

Use a comma after the greeting in a friendly letter.

Dear Tayo, Dear Aunt Claudia,

Use a comma after the closing in a letter.

Your friend, Yours truly,

Quotation Marks

See Quotations, p. 156.

GRAMMAR GUIDE

PROBLEM WORDS

Words	Rules	Examples
are our	*Are* is a verb. *Our* is a possessive pronoun.	Are these gloves yours? This is our car.
doesn't don't	Use *doesn't* with singular nouns, *he*, *she*, and *it*. Use *don't* with plural nouns, *I*, *you*, *we*, and *they*.	Dad doesn't swim. We don't swim.
good well	Use the adjective *good* to describe nouns. Use the adverb *well* to describe verbs.	The weather looks good. She sings well.
its it's	*Its* is a possessive pronoun. *It's* means "it is" (contraction).	The dog wagged its tail. It's cold today.
let leave	*Let* means "to allow." *Leave* means "to go away from" or "to let stay."	Please let me go swimming. I will leave soon. Leave it on my desk.
set sit	*Set* means "to put." *Sit* means "to rest or stay in one place."	Set the vase on the table. Please sit in this chair.
their there they're	*Their* means "belonging to them." *There* means "at or in that place." *They're* means "they are" (contraction).	Their coats are on the bed. Is Carlos there? They're going to the store.
two to too	*Two* is a number. *To* means "toward." *Too* means "also" or "more than enough."	I bought two shirts. A cat ran to the tree. Can we go too? I ate too many peas.
your you're	*Your* is a possessive pronoun. *You're* means "you are" (contraction).	Are these your glasses? You're late again!

ADVERB USAGE

Negatives

A negative word or negative contraction says "no" or "not." Do not use two negatives to express one negative idea.

Incorrect: We can't do nothing.
Correct: We can't do anything.
Correct: We can do nothing.

Negative Words		
no	nobody	nothing
never	none	nowhere
neither	no one	

PRONOUN USAGE

I and me

Use *I* as the subject of a sentence. Use *me* as an object pronoun and after words such as *to, with, for,* and *at*. Name yourself last when you talk about another person and yourself.

Beth and I are leaving for the beach. He will meet me.
Kwesi and I will practice. Give the directions to Roy and me.

MY NOTES

PROOFREADING CHECKLIST

Ask yourself each question. Check your paper for mistakes. Correct any mistakes you find. Put a check in the box when you find no more mistakes.

- ☐ **1.** Did I indent each paragraph?
- ☐ **2.** Does each sentence tell one complete thought?
- ☐ **3.** Did I end each sentence with the correct mark?
- ☐ **4.** Did I begin each sentence with a capital letter?
- ☐ **5.** Did I use capital letters correctly in other places?
- ☐ **6.** Did I use commas correctly?
- ☐ **7.** Did I spell all the words the right way?

Is there anything else you should look for? Make your own proofreading list.

- ☐ ____________________
- ☐ ____________________
- ☐ ____________________
- ☐ ____________________
- ☐ ____________________
- ☐ ____________________
- ☐ ____________________
- ☐ ____________________
- ☐ ____________________
- ☐ ____________________
- ☐ ____________________

PROOFREADING MARKS

Mark	Explanation	Example
¶	Begin a new paragraph. Indent the paragraph.	¶ We went to an air show last Saturday. Eight jets flew across the sky in the shape of V's, X's, and diamonds.
^	Add letters, words, or sentences.	The leaves were red ^and orange.
ℓ	Take out words, sentences, and punctuation marks. Correct spelling.	The sky is bright ~~blew.~~ blue Huge clouds ~~,~~ move quickly.
/	Change a capital letter to a small letter.	The /Fireflies blinked in the dark.
≡	Change a small letter to a capital letter.	New York city (≡) is exciting.